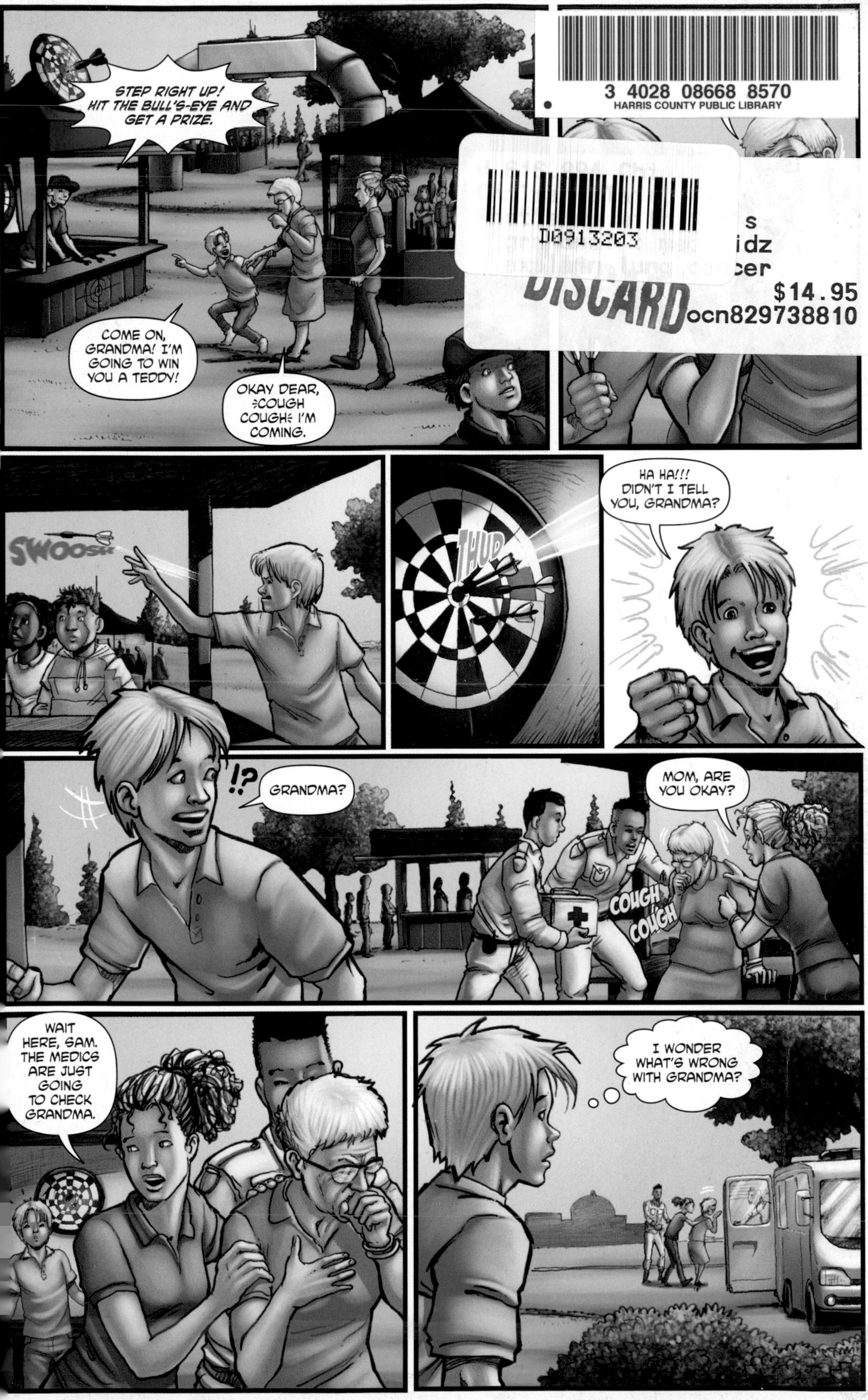
STEP RIGHT UP! HIT THE BULL'S-EYE AND GET A PRIZE.
COME ON, GRANDMA! I'M GOING TO WIN YOU A TEDDY!
OKAY DEAR, ⚡COUGH COUGH⚡ I'M COMING.
SWOOSH
THUD
HA HA!!! DIDN'T I TELL YOU, GRANDMA?
!?
GRANDMA?
MOM, ARE YOU OKAY?
COUGH
COUGH
WAIT HERE, SAM. THE MEDICS ARE JUST GOING TO CHECK GRANDMA.
I WONDER WHAT'S WRONG WITH GRANDMA?

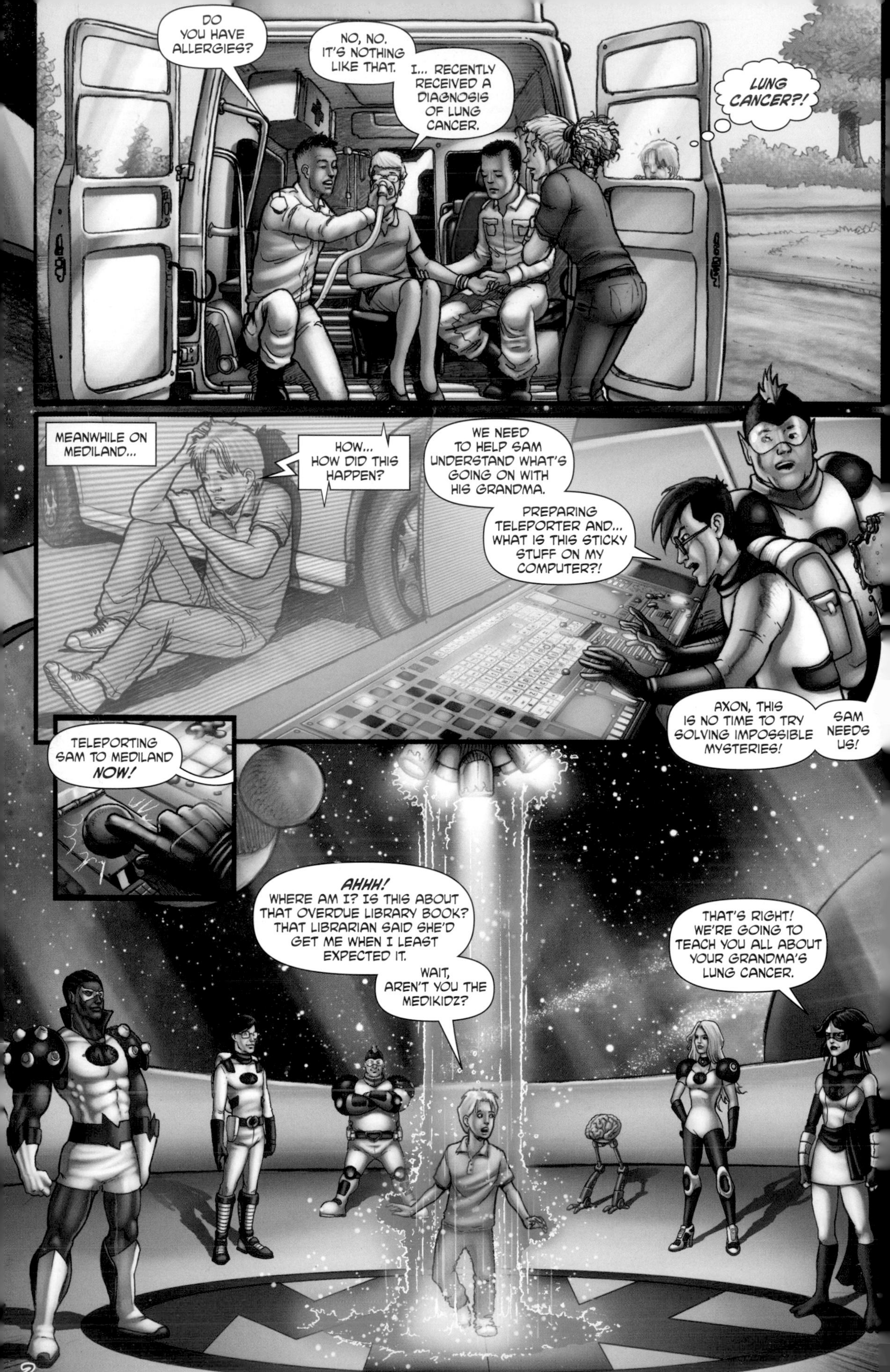
DO YOU HAVE ALLERGIES?
NO, NO. IT'S NOTHING LIKE THAT.
I... RECENTLY RECEIVED A DIAGNOSIS OF LUNG CANCER.
LUNG CANCER?!
MEANWHILE ON MEDILAND...
HOW... HOW DID THIS HAPPEN?
WE NEED TO HELP SAM UNDERSTAND WHAT'S GOING ON WITH HIS GRANDMA.
PREPARING TELEPORTER AND... WHAT IS THIS STICKY STUFF ON MY COMPUTER?!
AXON, THIS IS NO TIME TO TRY SOLVING IMPOSSIBLE MYSTERIES!
SAM NEEDS US!
TELEPORTING SAM TO MEDILAND NOW!
AHHH! WHERE AM I? IS THIS ABOUT THAT OVERDUE LIBRARY BOOK? THAT LIBRARIAN SAID SHE'D GET ME WHEN I LEAST EXPECTED IT.
WAIT, AREN'T YOU THE MEDIKIDZ?
THAT'S RIGHT! WE'RE GOING TO TEACH YOU ALL ABOUT YOUR GRANDMA'S LUNG CANCER.

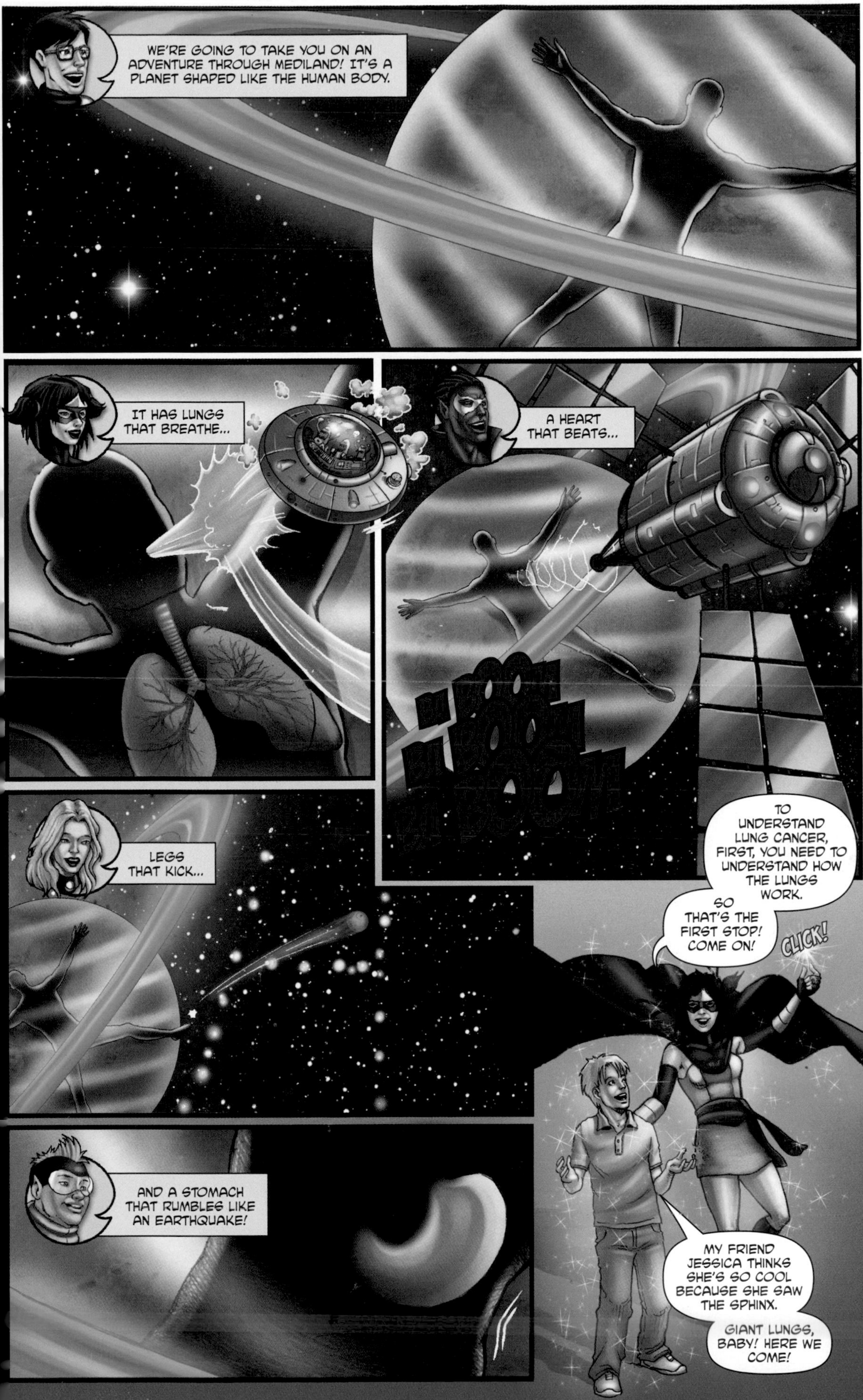
WE'RE GOING TO TAKE YOU ON AN ADVENTURE THROUGH MEDILAND! IT'S A PLANET SHAPED LIKE THE HUMAN BODY.
IT HAS LUNGS THAT BREATHE...
A HEART THAT BEATS...
LEGS THAT KICK...
AND A STOMACH THAT RUMBLES LIKE AN EARTHQUAKE!
TO UNDERSTAND LUNG CANCER, FIRST, YOU NEED TO UNDERSTAND HOW THE LUNGS WORK.
SO THAT'S THE FIRST STOP! COME ON!
CLICK!
MY FRIEND JESSICA THINKS SHE'S SO COOL BECAUSE SHE SAW THE SPHINX.
GIANT LUNGS, BABY! HERE WE COME!

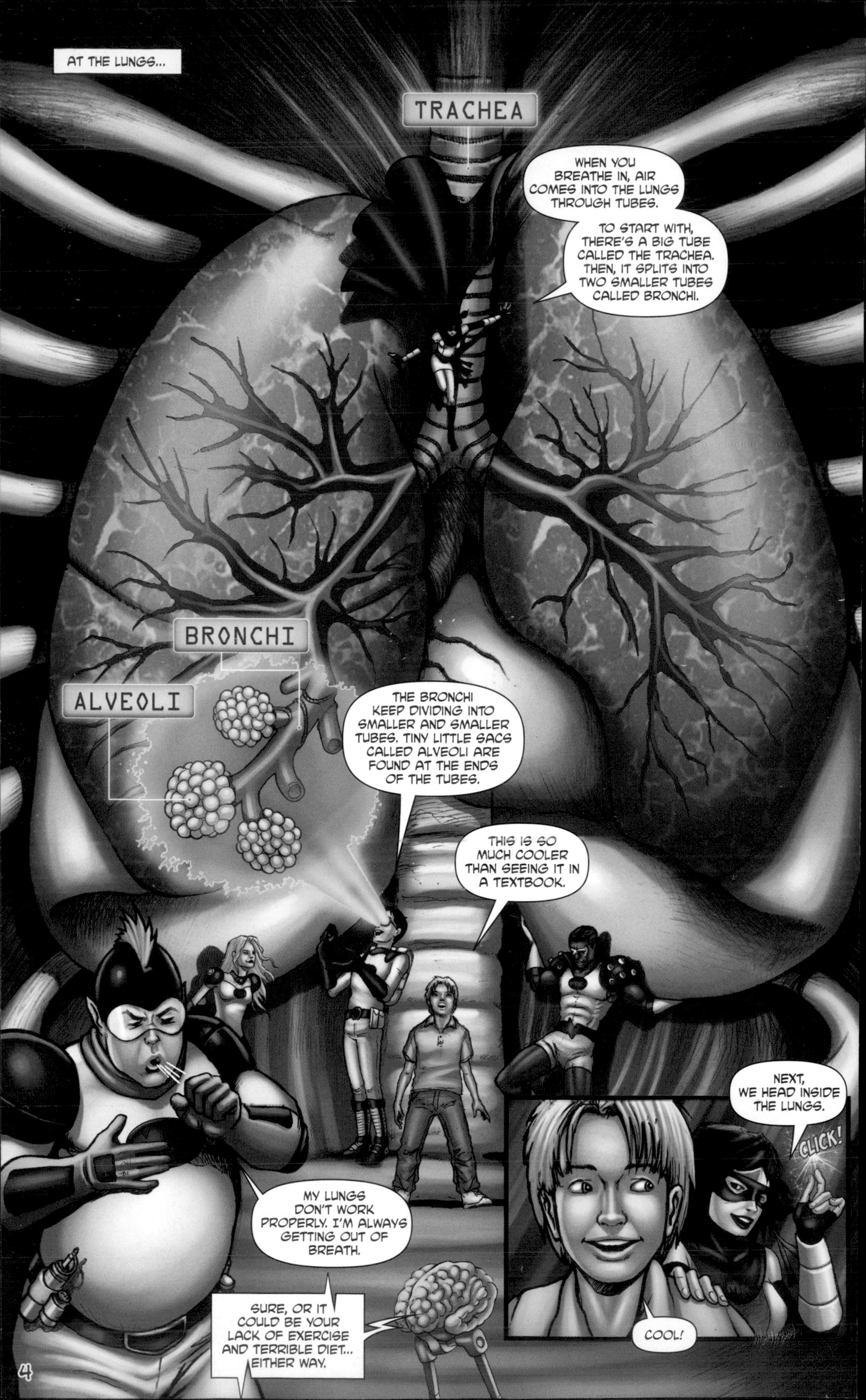

AT THE LUNGS...
TRACHEA
WHEN YOU BREATHE IN, AIR COMES INTO THE LUNGS THROUGH TUBES.
TO START WITH, THERE'S A BIG TUBE CALLED THE TRACHEA. THEN, IT SPLITS INTO TWO SMALLER TUBES CALLED BRONCHI.
BRONCHI
ALVEOLI
THE BRONCHI KEEP DIVIDING INTO SMALLER AND SMALLER TUBES. TINY LITTLE SACS CALLED ALVEOLI ARE FOUND AT THE ENDS OF THE TUBES.
THIS IS SO MUCH COOLER THAN SEEING IT IN A TEXTBOOK.
MY LUNGS DON'T WORK PROPERLY. I'M ALWAYS GETTING OUT OF BREATH.
SURE, OR IT COULD BE YOUR LACK OF EXERCISE AND TERRIBLE DIET... EITHER WAY.
NEXT, WE HEAD INSIDE THE LUNGS.
CLICK!
COOL!

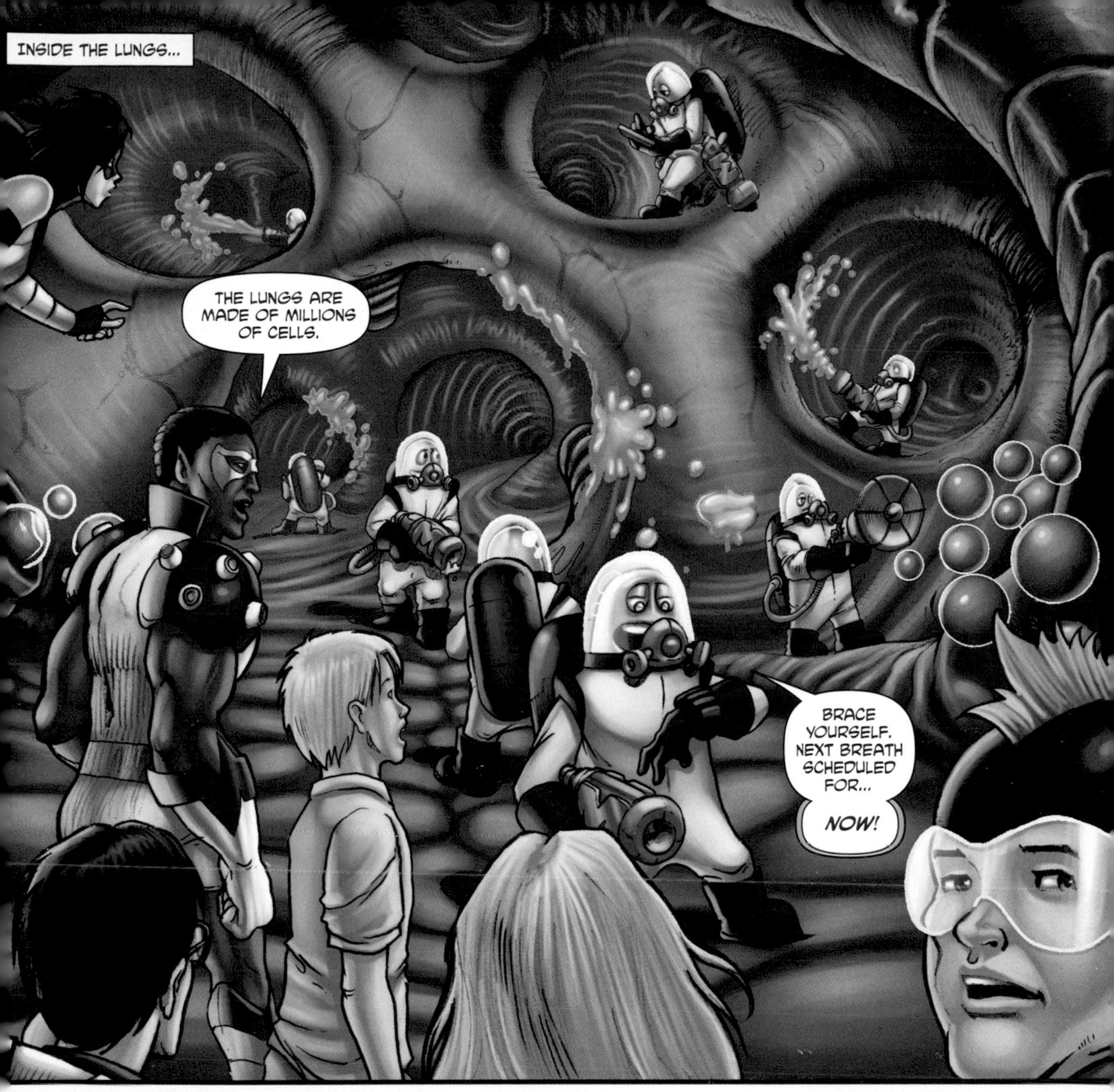

INSIDE THE LUNGS...
THE LUNGS ARE MADE OF MILLIONS OF CELLS.
BRACE YOURSELF. NEXT BREATH SCHEDULED FOR...
NOW!

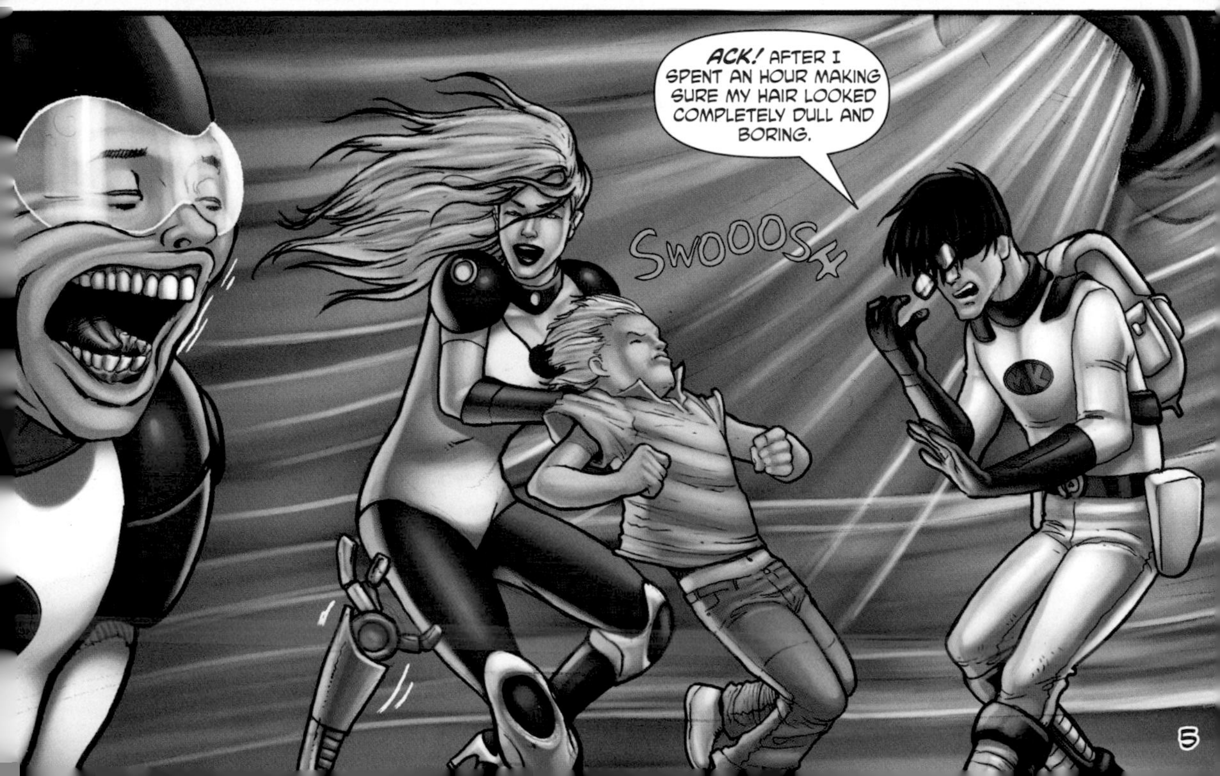

ACK! AFTER I SPENT AN HOUR MAKING SURE MY HAIR LOOKED COMPLETELY DULL AND BORING.
SWOOOSH

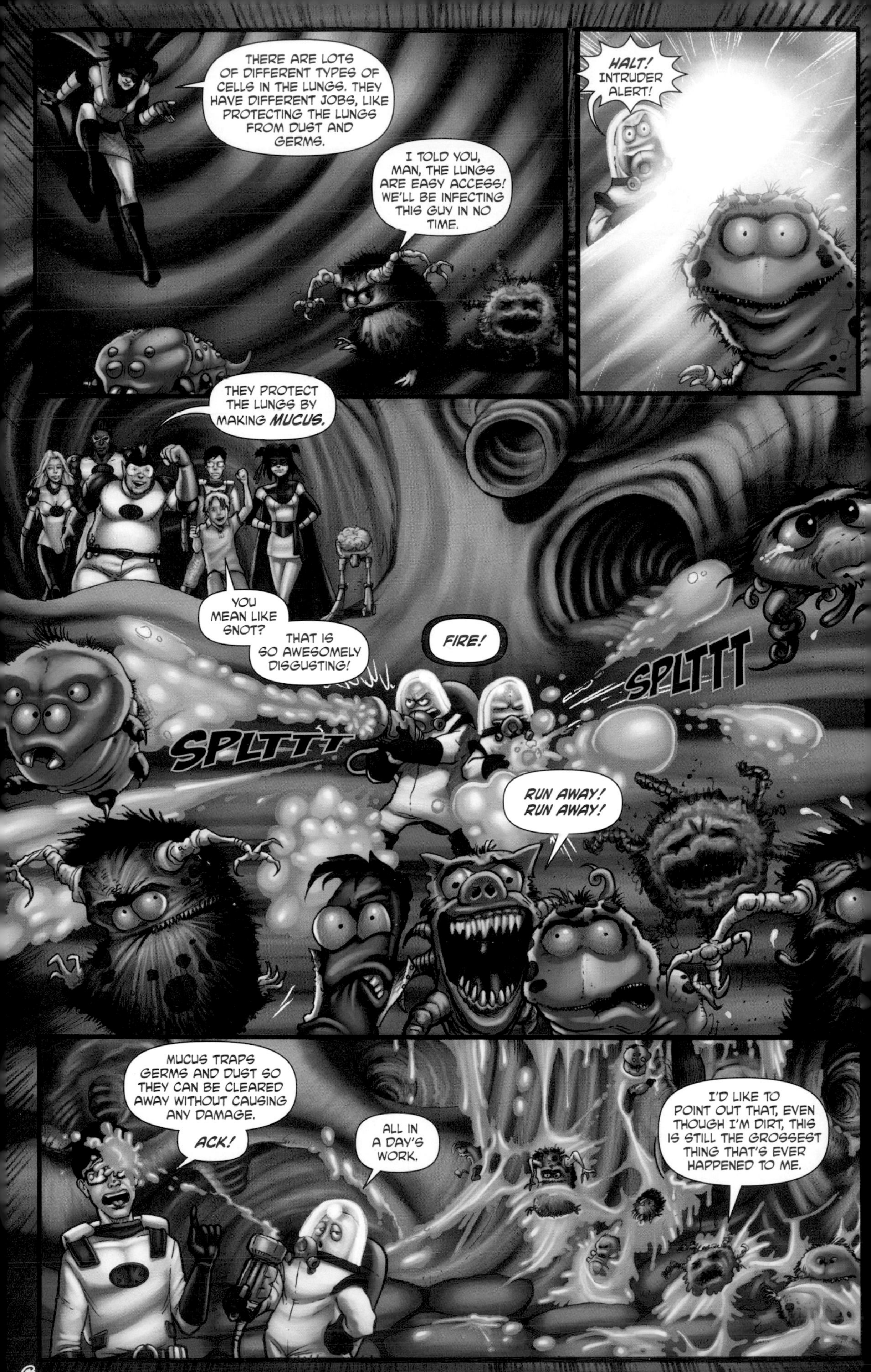
THERE ARE LOTS OF DIFFERENT TYPES OF CELLS IN THE LUNGS. THEY HAVE DIFFERENT JOBS, LIKE PROTECTING THE LUNGS FROM DUST AND GERMS.
I TOLD YOU, MAN, THE LUNGS ARE EASY ACCESS! WE'LL BE INFECTING THIS GUY IN NO TIME.
HALT! INTRUDER ALERT!
THEY PROTECT THE LUNGS BY MAKING MUCUS.
YOU MEAN LIKE SNOT?
THAT IS SO AWESOMELY DISGUSTING!
FIRE!
SPLTTT
SPLTTT
RUN AWAY! RUN AWAY!
MUCUS TRAPS GERMS AND DUST SO THEY CAN BE CLEARED AWAY WITHOUT CAUSING ANY DAMAGE.
ACK!
ALL IN A DAY'S WORK.
I'D LIKE TO POINT OUT THAT, EVEN THOUGH I'M DIRT, THIS IS STILL THE GROSSEST THING THAT'S EVER HAPPENED TO ME.

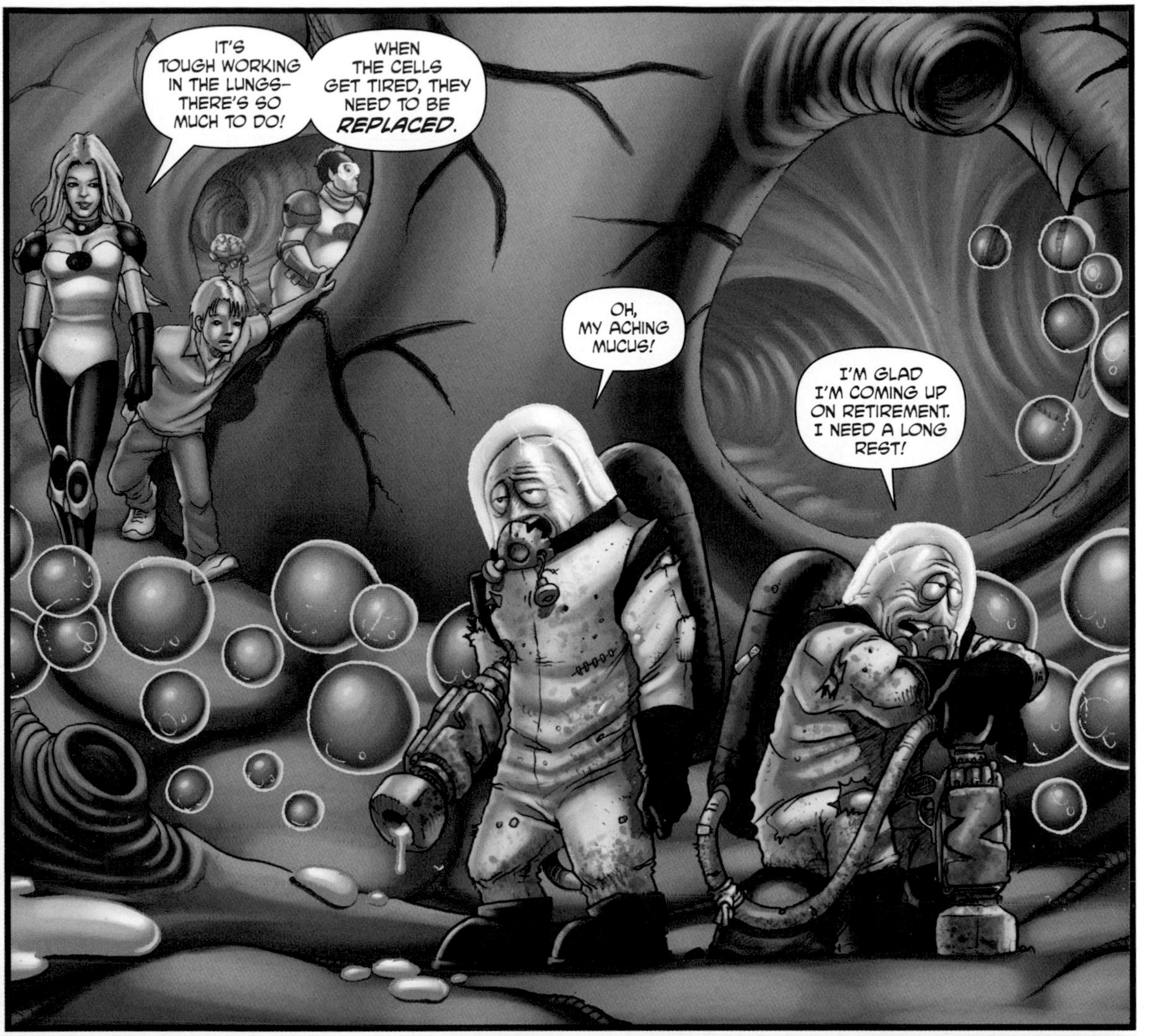
IT'S TOUGH WORKING IN THE LUNGS– THERE'S SO MUCH TO DO!
WHEN THE CELLS GET TIRED, THEY NEED TO BE *REPLACED*.
OH, MY ACHING MUCUS!
I'M GLAD I'M COMING UP ON RETIREMENT. I NEED A LONG REST!

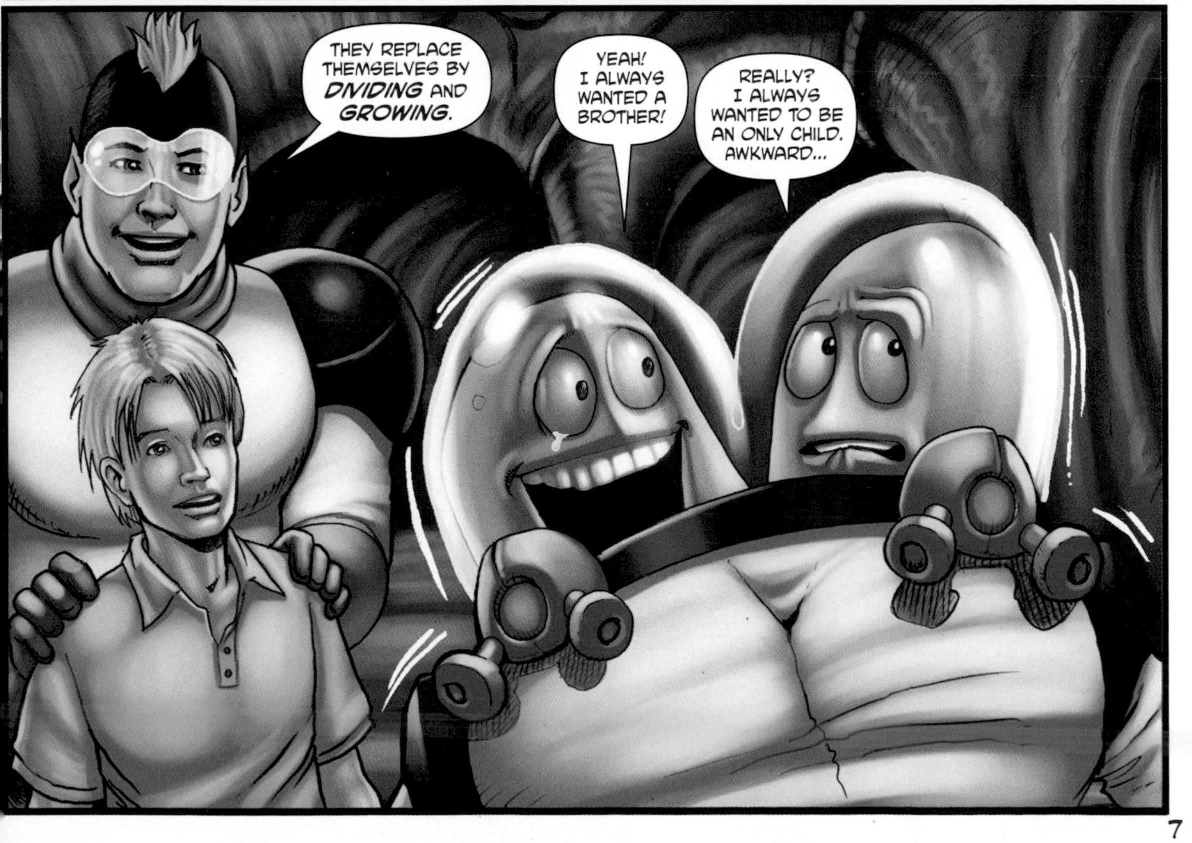
THEY REPLACE THEMSELVES BY *DIVIDING* AND *GROWING*.
YEAH! I ALWAYS WANTED A BROTHER!
REALLY? I ALWAYS WANTED TO BE AN ONLY CHILD. AWKWARD...

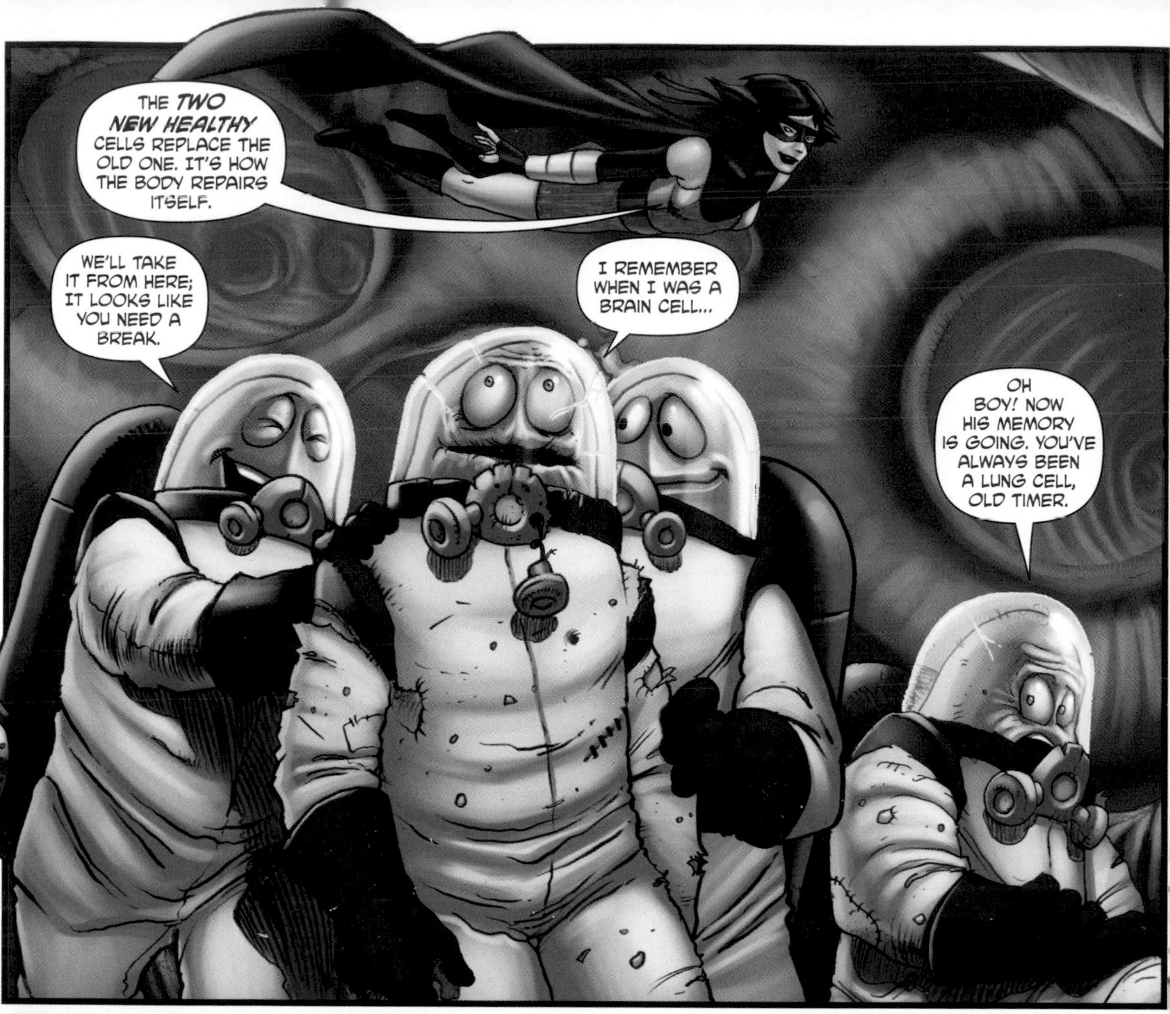
THE TWO NEW HEALTHY CELLS REPLACE THE OLD ONE. IT'S HOW THE BODY REPAIRS ITSELF.
WE'LL TAKE IT FROM HERE; IT LOOKS LIKE YOU NEED A BREAK.
I REMEMBER WHEN I WAS A BRAIN CELL...
OH BOY! NOW HIS MEMORY IS GOING. YOU'VE ALWAYS BEEN A LUNG CELL, OLD TIMER.

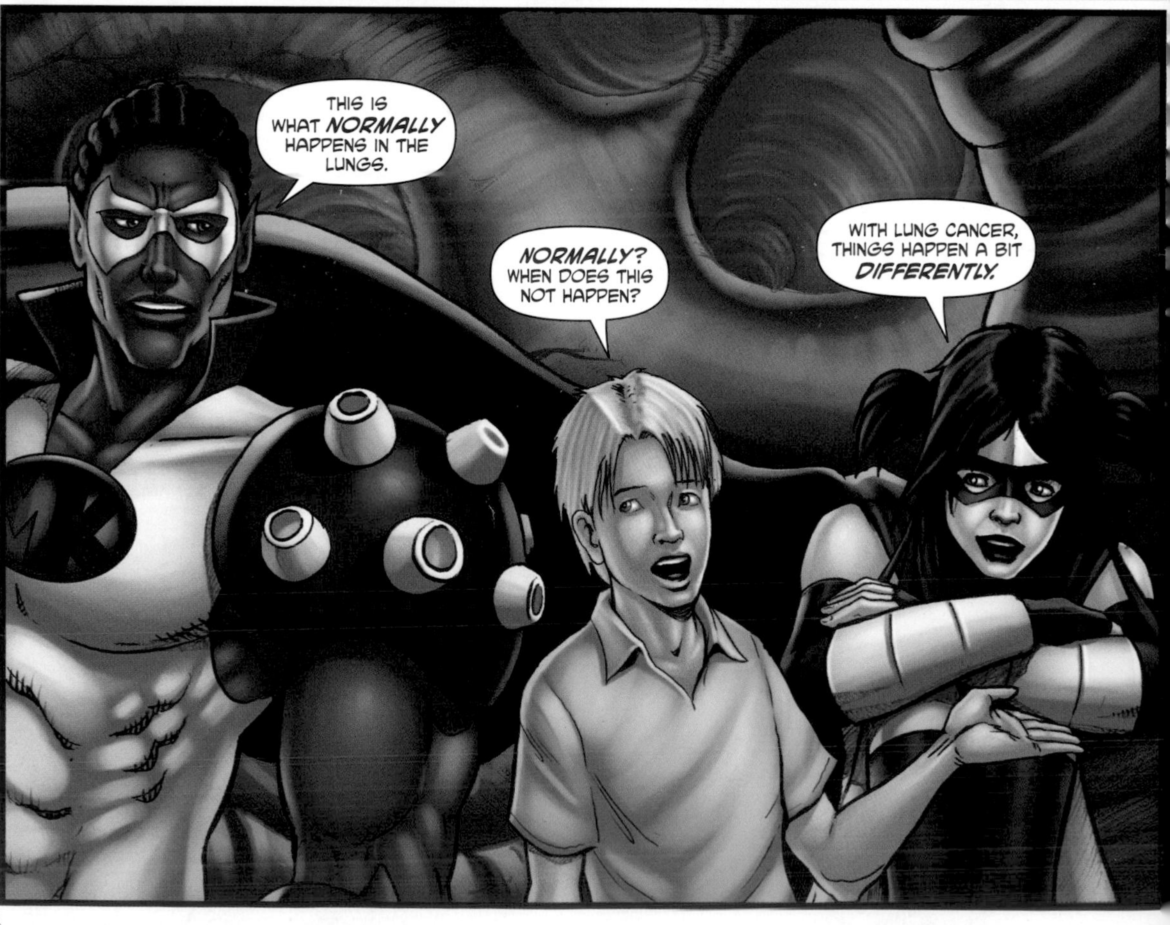
THIS IS WHAT NORMALLY HAPPENS IN THE LUNGS.
NORMALLY? WHEN DOES THIS NOT HAPPEN?
WITH LUNG CANCER, THINGS HAPPEN A BIT DIFFERENTLY.

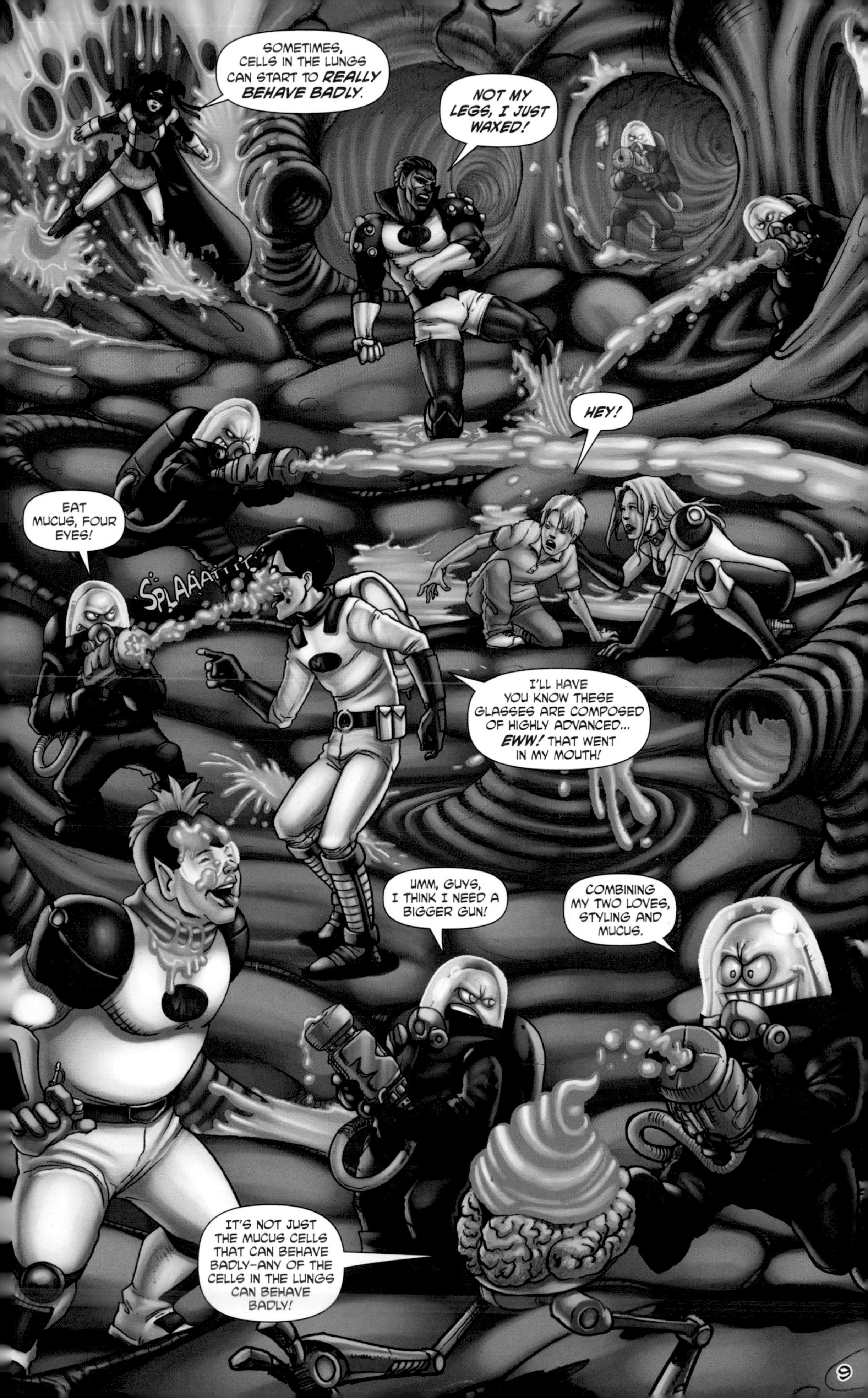
SOMETIMES, CELLS IN THE LUNGS CAN START TO REALLY BEHAVE BADLY.
NOT MY LEGS, I JUST WAXED!
HEY!
EAT MUCUS, FOUR EYES!
SPLAAATTT
I'LL HAVE YOU KNOW THESE GLASSES ARE COMPOSED OF HIGHLY ADVANCED... EWW! THAT WENT IN MY MOUTH!
UMM, GUYS, I THINK I NEED A BIGGER GUN!
COMBINING MY TWO LOVES, STYLING AND MUCUS.
IT'S NOT JUST THE MUCUS CELLS THAT CAN BEHAVE BADLY–ANY OF THE CELLS IN THE LUNGS CAN BEHAVE BADLY!

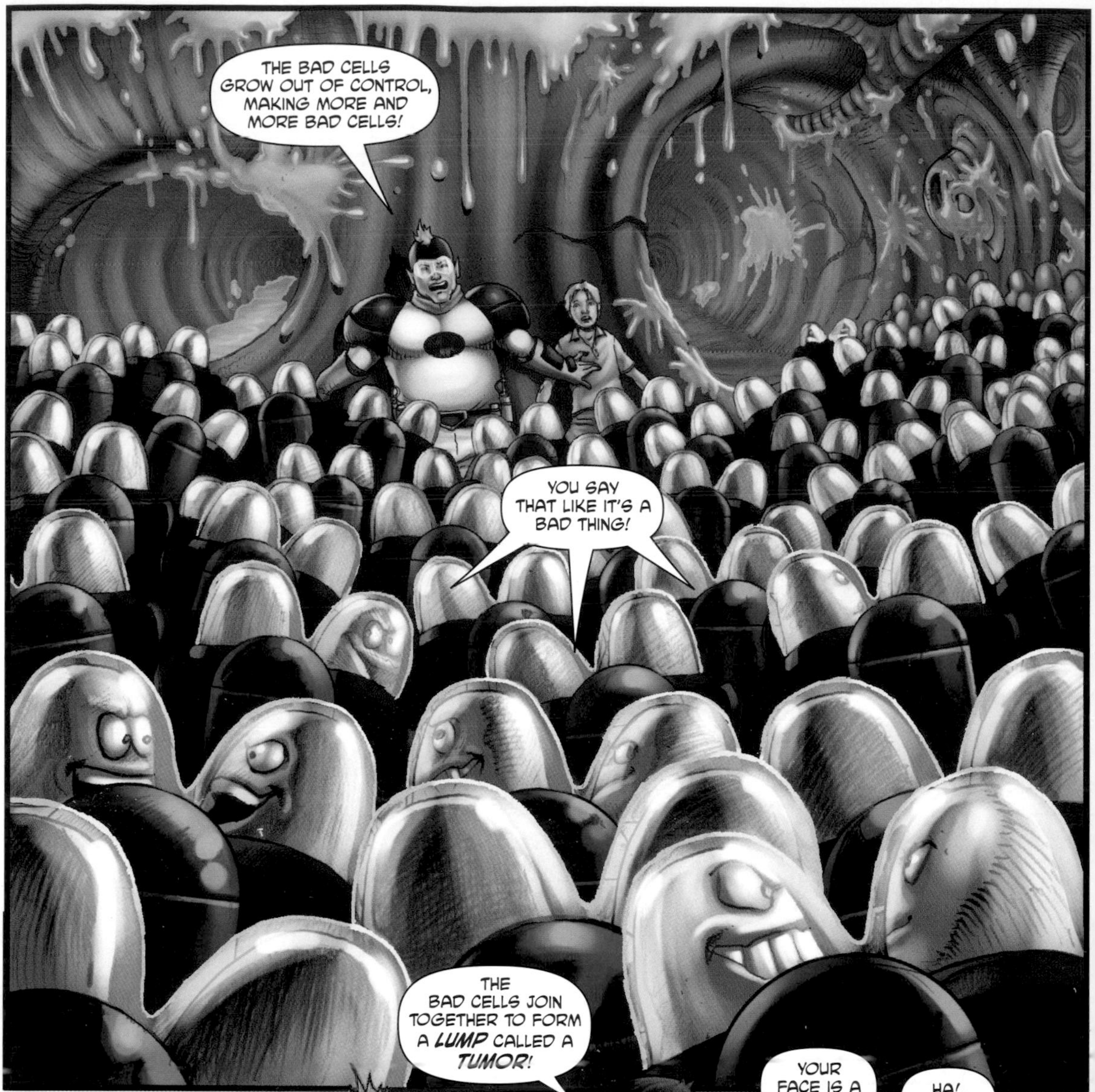
THE BAD CELLS GROW OUT OF CONTROL, MAKING MORE AND MORE BAD CELLS!
YOU SAY THAT LIKE IT'S A BAD THING!

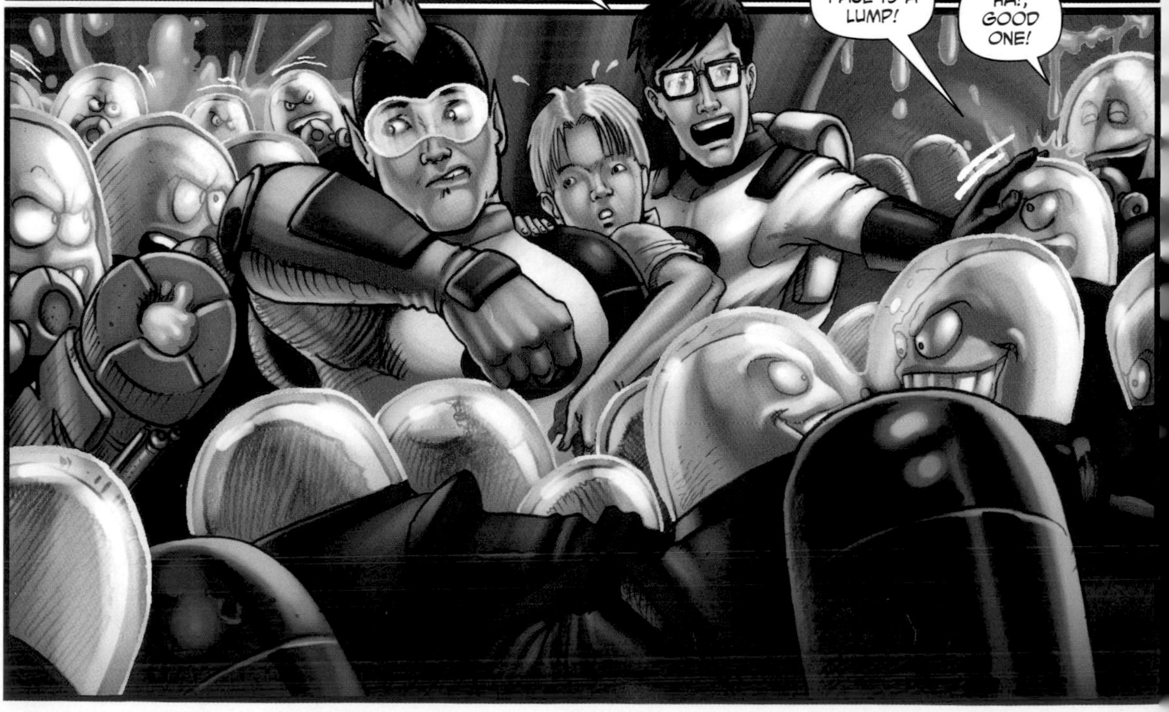
THE BAD CELLS JOIN TOGETHER TO FORM A ***LUMP*** CALLED A ***TUMOR***!
YOUR FACE IS A LUMP!
HA!, GOOD ONE!

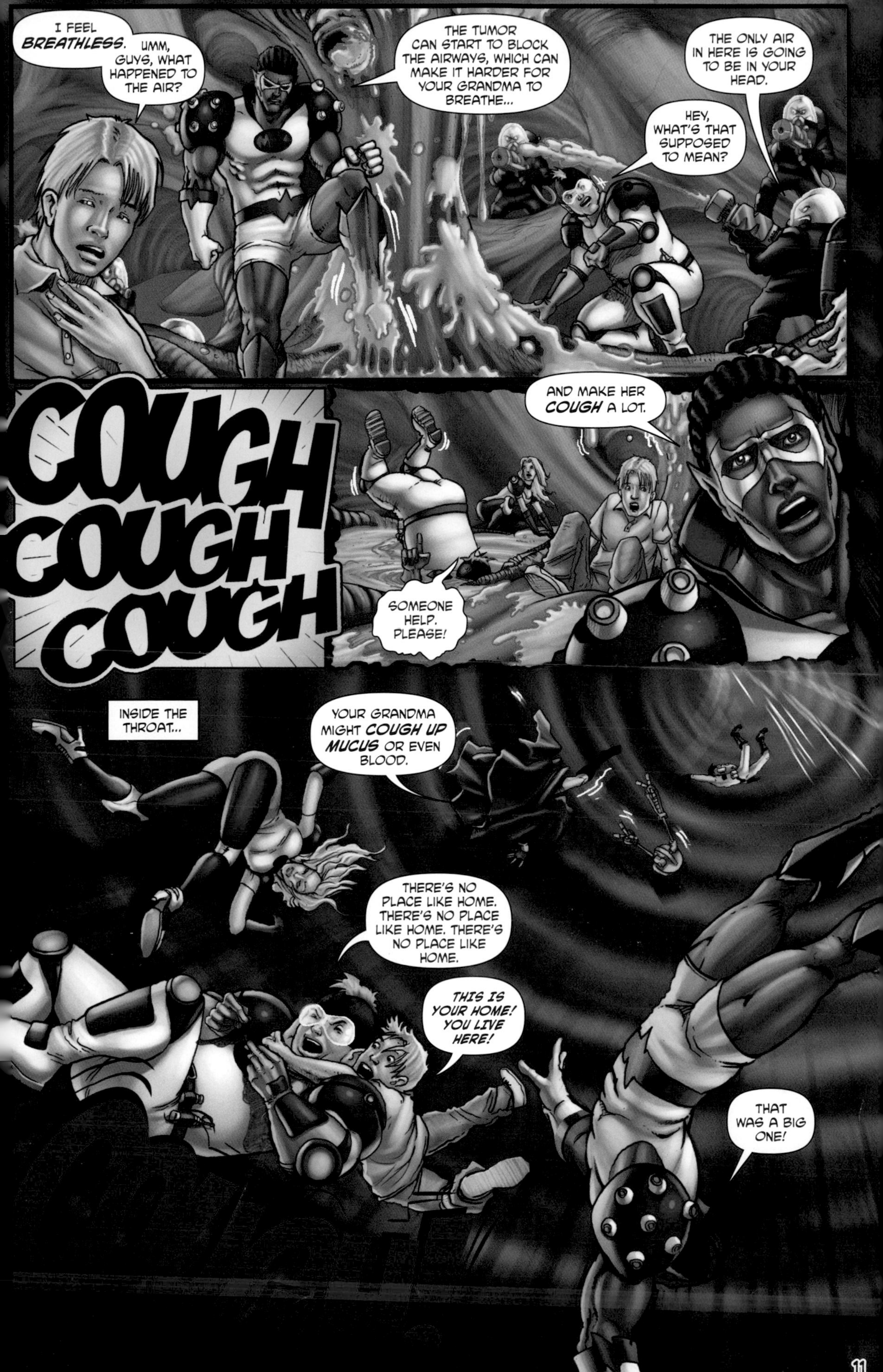

I FEEL BREATHLESS. UMM, GUYS, WHAT HAPPENED TO THE AIR?
THE TUMOR CAN START TO BLOCK THE AIRWAYS, WHICH CAN MAKE IT HARDER FOR YOUR GRANDMA TO BREATHE...
THE ONLY AIR IN HERE IS GOING TO BE IN YOUR HEAD.
HEY, WHAT'S THAT SUPPOSED TO MEAN?
COUGH COUGH COUGH
AND MAKE HER COUGH A LOT.
SOMEONE HELP. PLEASE!
INSIDE THE THROAT...
YOUR GRANDMA MIGHT COUGH UP MUCUS OR EVEN BLOOD.
THERE'S NO PLACE LIKE HOME. THERE'S NO PLACE LIKE HOME. THERE'S NO PLACE LIKE HOME.
THIS IS YOUR HOME! YOU LIVE HERE!
THAT WAS A BIG ONE!

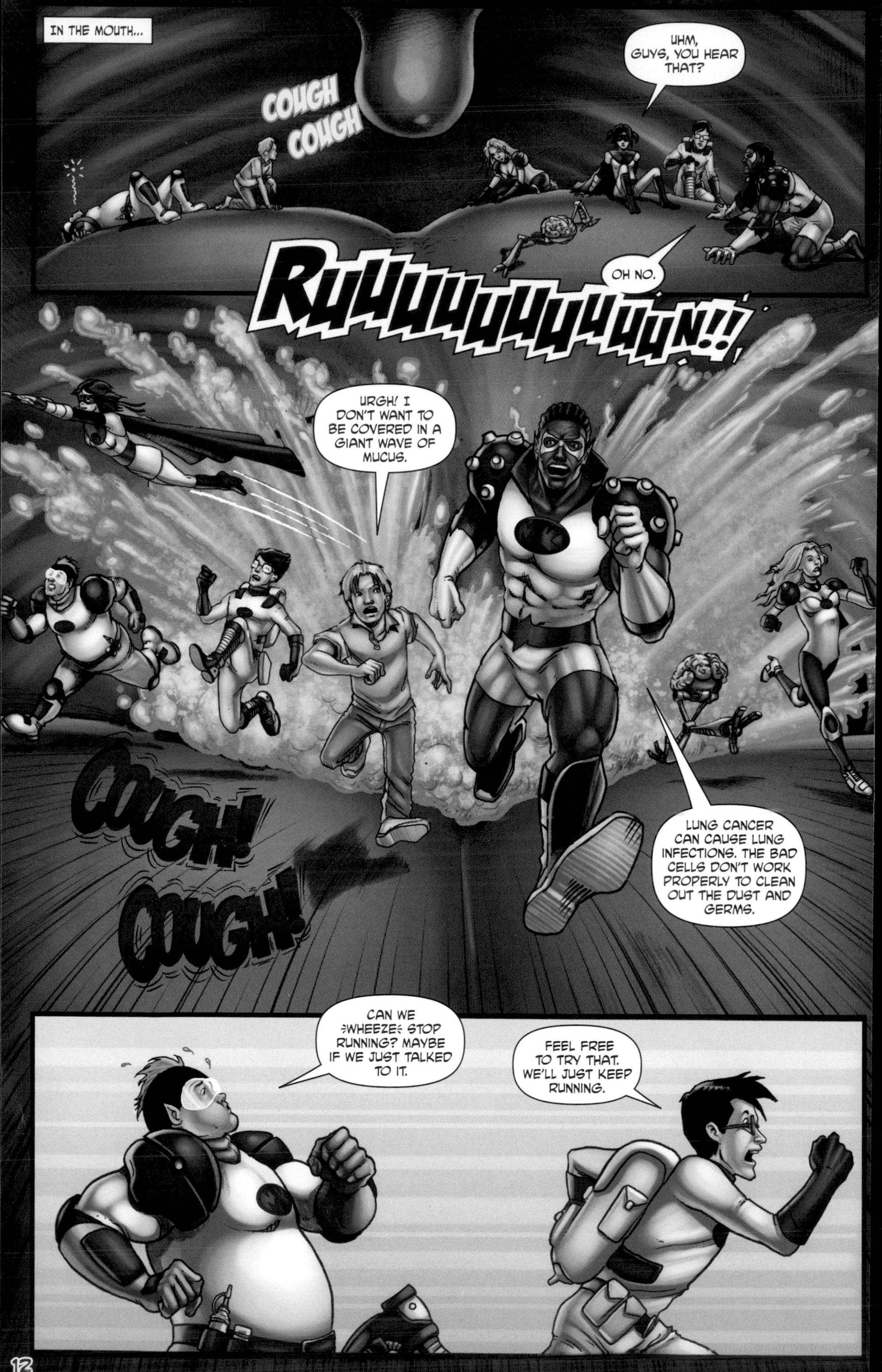
IN THE MOUTH...
COUGH COUGH
UHM, GUYS, YOU HEAR THAT?
OH NO.
RUUUUUUUUUUN!!
URGH! I DON'T WANT TO BE COVERED IN A GIANT WAVE OF MUCUS.
LUNG CANCER CAN CAUSE LUNG INFECTIONS. THE BAD CELLS DON'T WORK PROPERLY TO CLEAN OUT THE DUST AND GERMS.
COUGH! COUGH!
CAN WE ≑WHEEZE≑ STOP RUNNING? MAYBE IF WE JUST TALKED TO IT.
FEEL FREE TO TRY THAT. WE'LL JUST KEEP RUNNING.

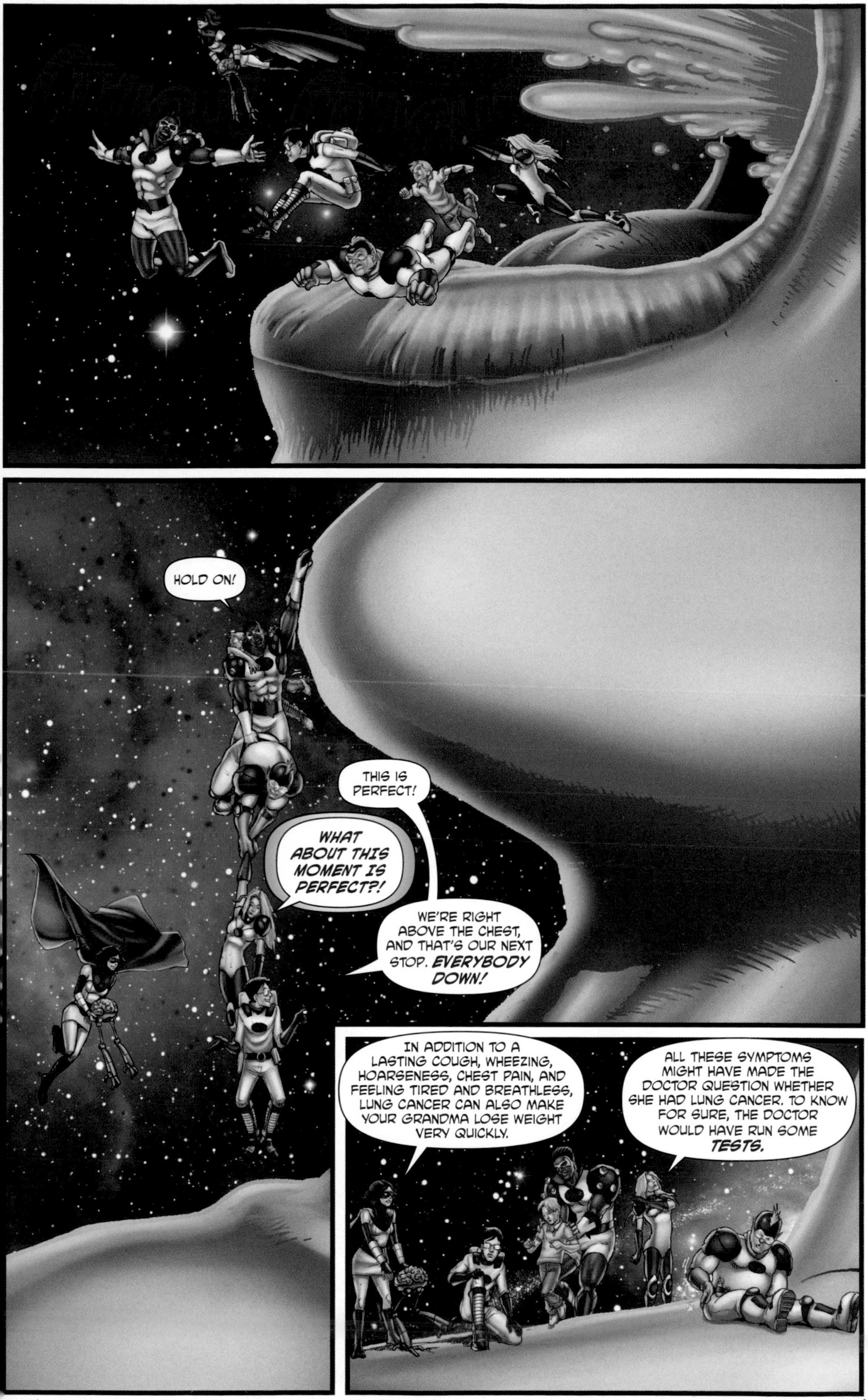
HOLD ON!
THIS IS PERFECT!
WHAT ABOUT THIS MOMENT IS PERFECT?!
WE'RE RIGHT ABOVE THE CHEST, AND THAT'S OUR NEXT STOP. EVERYBODY DOWN!
IN ADDITION TO A LASTING COUGH, WHEEZING, HOARSENESS, CHEST PAIN, AND FEELING TIRED AND BREATHLESS, LUNG CANCER CAN ALSO MAKE YOUR GRANDMA LOSE WEIGHT VERY QUICKLY.
ALL THESE SYMPTOMS MIGHT HAVE MADE THE DOCTOR QUESTION WHETHER SHE HAD LUNG CANCER. TO KNOW FOR SURE, THE DOCTOR WOULD HAVE RUN SOME TESTS.

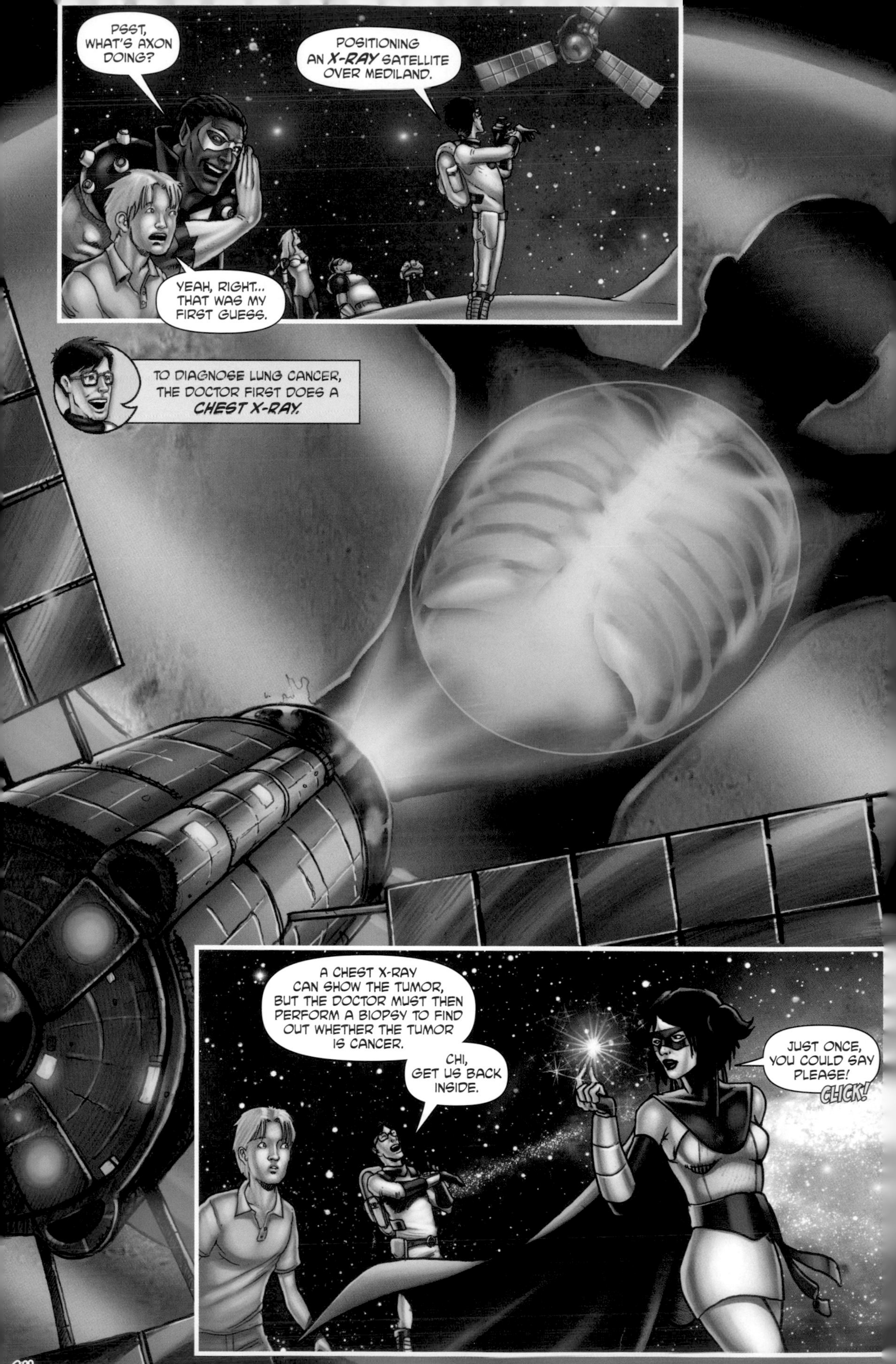
PSST, WHAT'S AXON DOING?
POSITIONING AN X-RAY SATELLITE OVER MEDILAND.
YEAH, RIGHT... THAT WAS MY FIRST GUESS.
TO DIAGNOSE LUNG CANCER, THE DOCTOR FIRST DOES A CHEST X-RAY.
A CHEST X-RAY CAN SHOW THE TUMOR, BUT THE DOCTOR MUST THEN PERFORM A BIOPSY TO FIND OUT WHETHER THE TUMOR IS CANCER.
CHI, GET US BACK INSIDE.
JUST ONCE, YOU COULD SAY PLEASE!
CLICK!

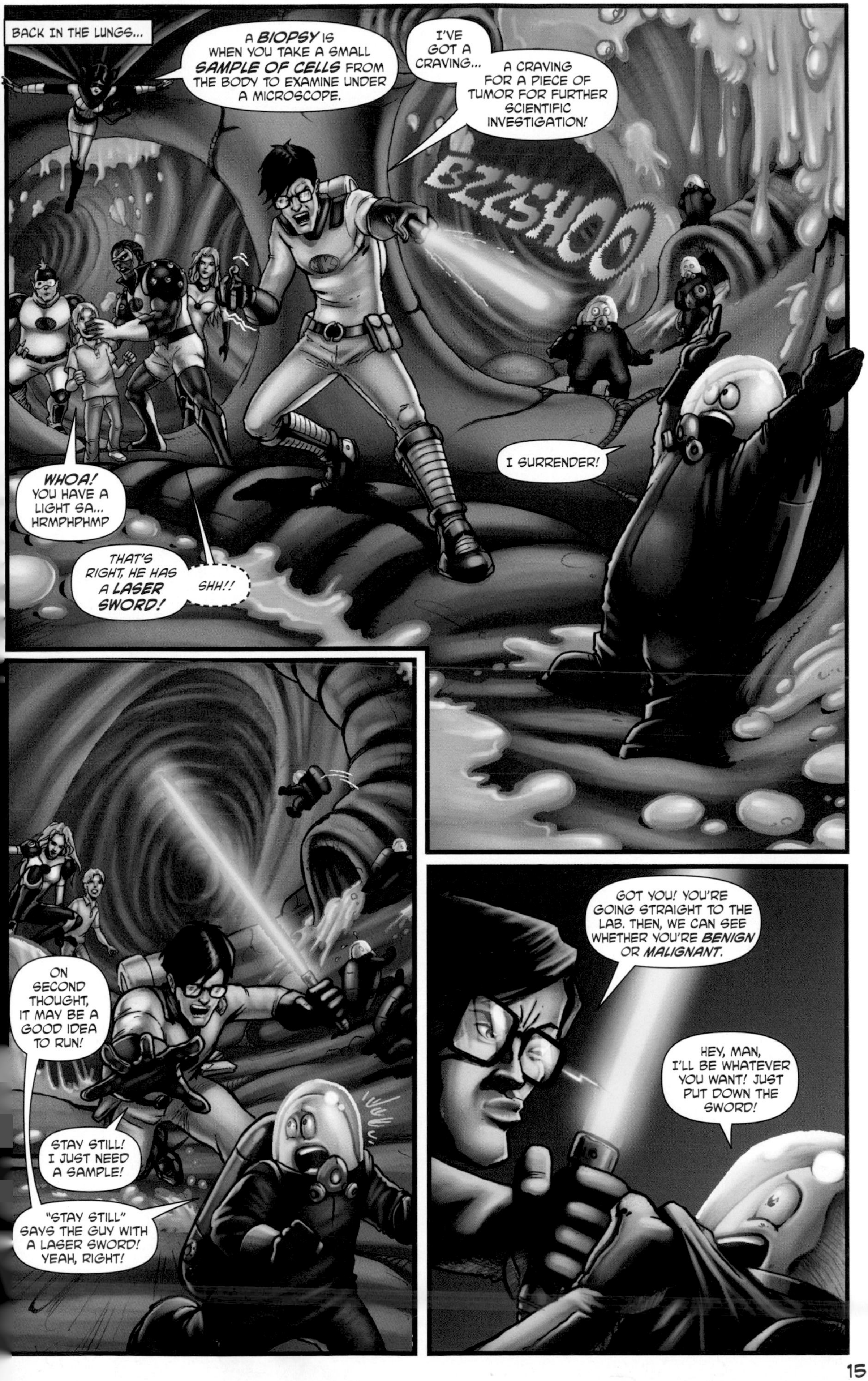
BACK IN THE LUNGS...
A BIOPSY IS WHEN YOU TAKE A SMALL SAMPLE OF CELLS FROM THE BODY TO EXAMINE UNDER A MICROSCOPE.
I'VE GOT A CRAVING...
A CRAVING FOR A PIECE OF TUMOR FOR FURTHER SCIENTIFIC INVESTIGATION!
BZSHOO
I SURRENDER!
WHOA! YOU HAVE A LIGHT SA... HRMPHPHMP
THAT'S RIGHT, HE HAS A LASER SWORD!
SHH!!
ON SECOND THOUGHT, IT MAY BE A GOOD IDEA TO RUN!
STAY STILL! I JUST NEED A SAMPLE!
"STAY STILL" SAYS THE GUY WITH A LASER SWORD! YEAH, RIGHT!
GOT YOU! YOU'RE GOING STRAIGHT TO THE LAB. THEN, WE CAN SEE WHETHER YOU'RE BENIGN OR MALIGNANT.
HEY, MAN, I'LL BE WHATEVER YOU WANT! JUST PUT DOWN THE SWORD!

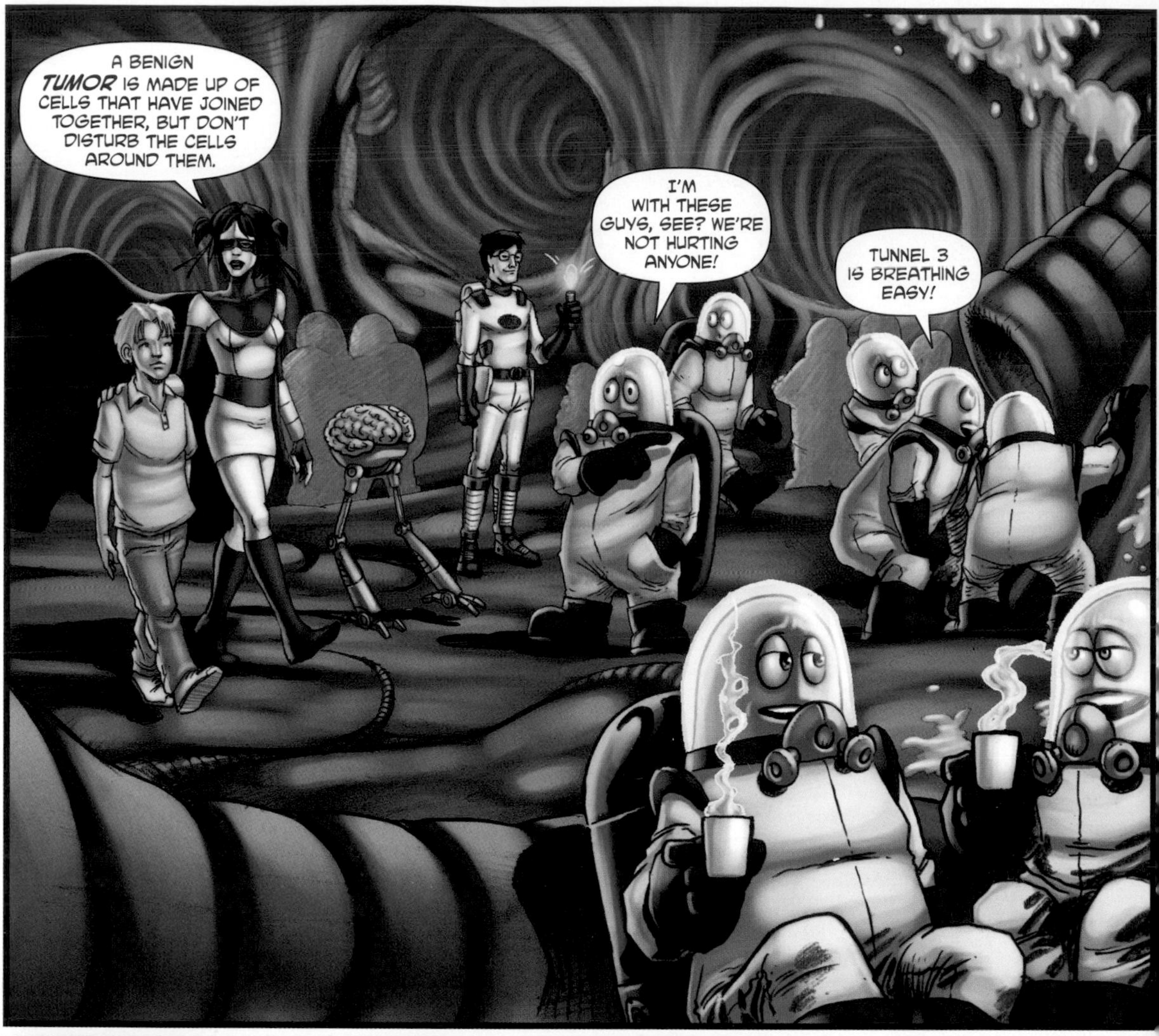
A BENIGN TUMOR IS MADE UP OF CELLS THAT HAVE JOINED TOGETHER, BUT DON'T DISTURB THE CELLS AROUND THEM.
I'M WITH THESE GUYS, SEE? WE'RE NOT HURTING ANYONE!
TUNNEL 3 IS BREATHING EASY!

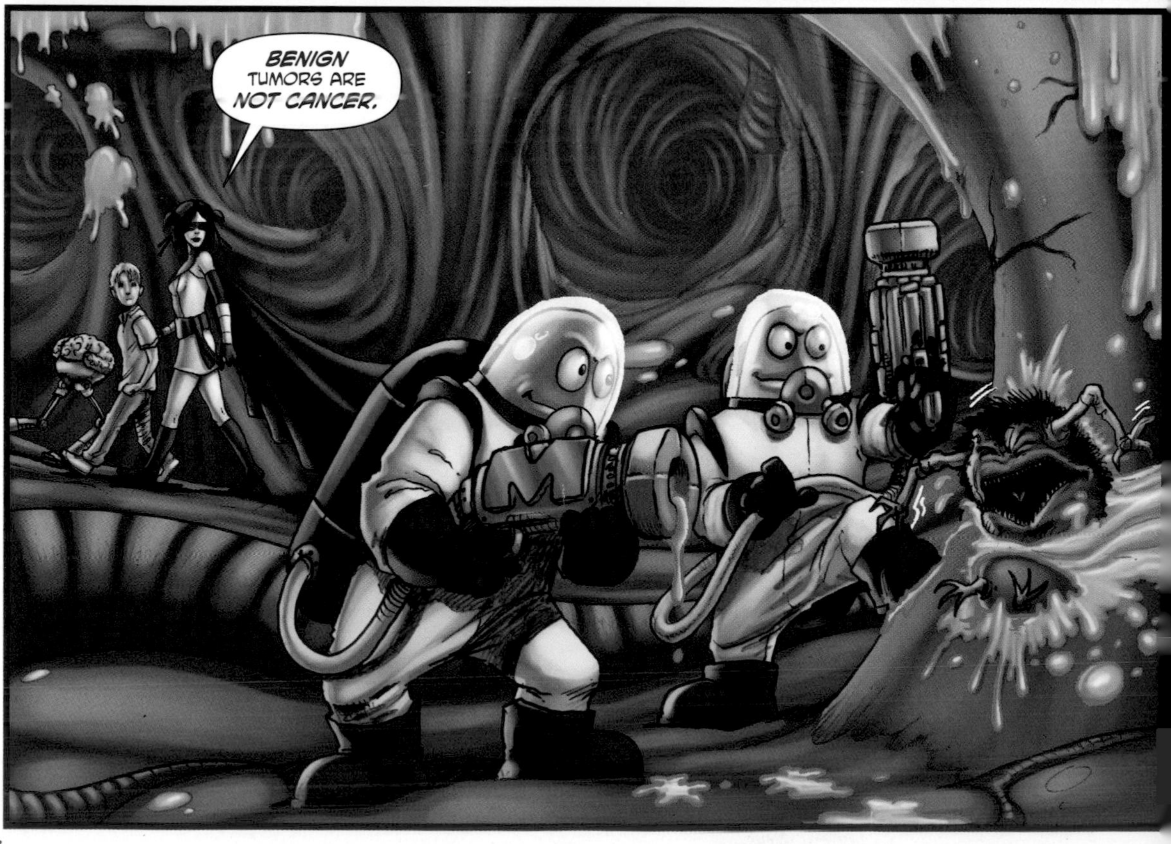
BENIGN TUMORS ARE NOT CANCER.

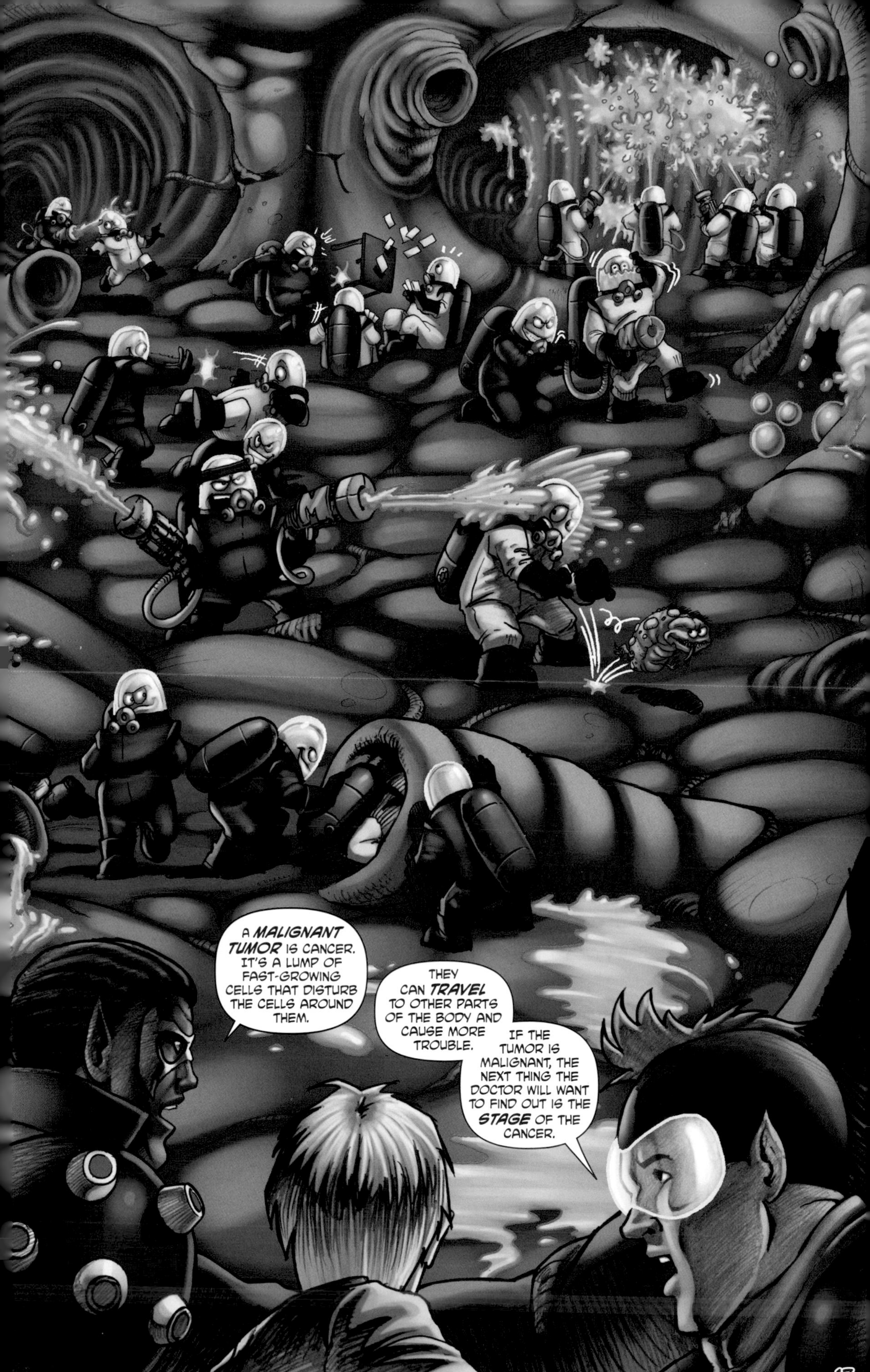
A MALIGNANT TUMOR IS CANCER. IT'S A LUMP OF FAST-GROWING CELLS THAT DISTURB THE CELLS AROUND THEM.
THEY CAN TRAVEL TO OTHER PARTS OF THE BODY AND CAUSE MORE TROUBLE.
IF THE TUMOR IS MALIGNANT, THE NEXT THING THE DOCTOR WILL WANT TO FIND OUT IS THE STAGE OF THE CANCER.

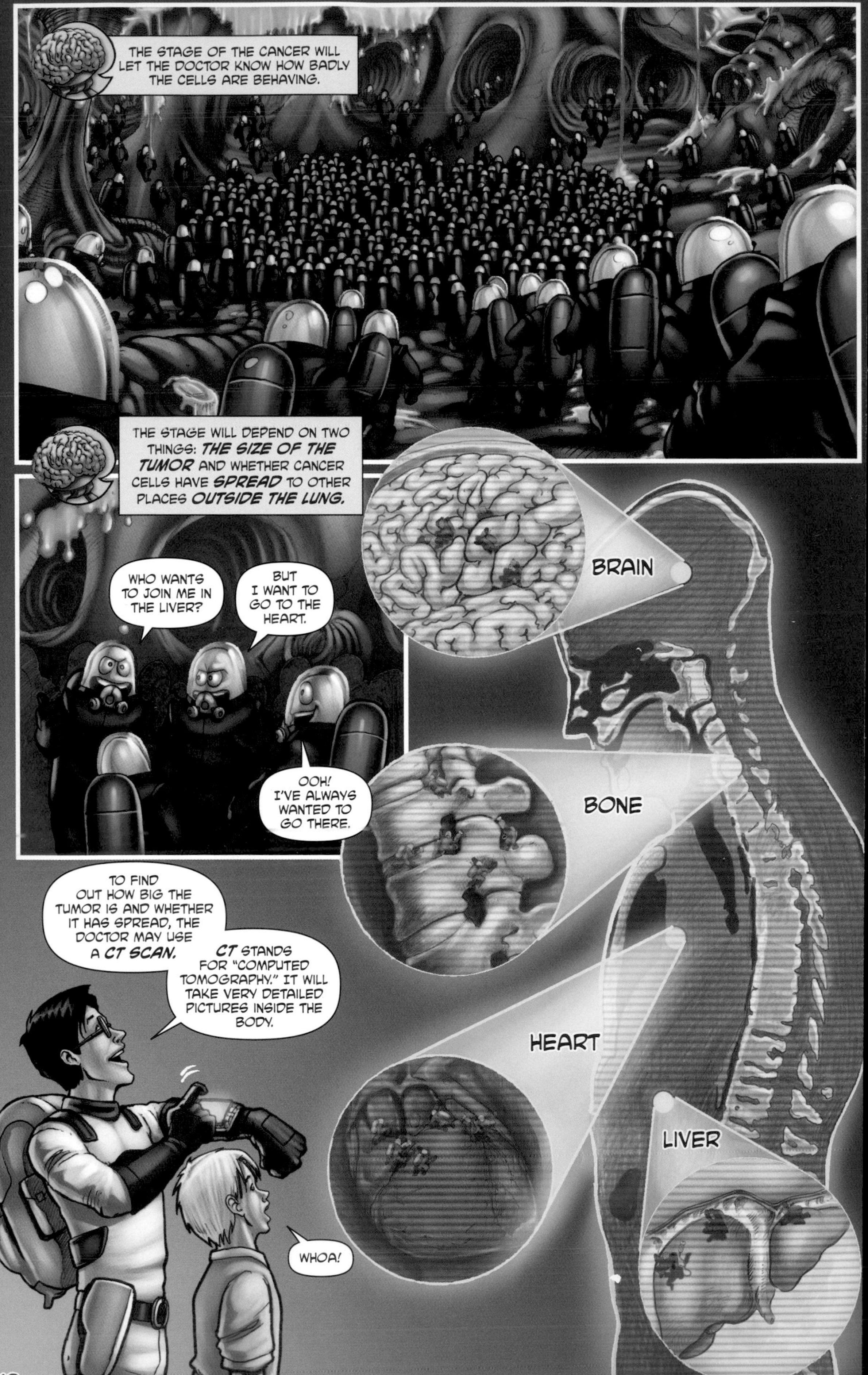
THE STAGE OF THE CANCER WILL LET THE DOCTOR KNOW HOW BADLY THE CELLS ARE BEHAVING.
THE STAGE WILL DEPEND ON TWO THINGS: THE SIZE OF THE TUMOR AND WHETHER CANCER CELLS HAVE SPREAD TO OTHER PLACES OUTSIDE THE LUNG.
WHO WANTS TO JOIN ME IN THE LIVER?
BUT I WANT TO GO TO THE HEART.
OOH! I'VE ALWAYS WANTED TO GO THERE.
BRAIN
BONE
HEART
LIVER
TO FIND OUT HOW BIG THE TUMOR IS AND WHETHER IT HAS SPREAD, THE DOCTOR MAY USE A CT SCAN.
CT STANDS FOR "COMPUTED TOMOGRAPHY." IT WILL TAKE VERY DETAILED PICTURES INSIDE THE BODY.
WHOA!

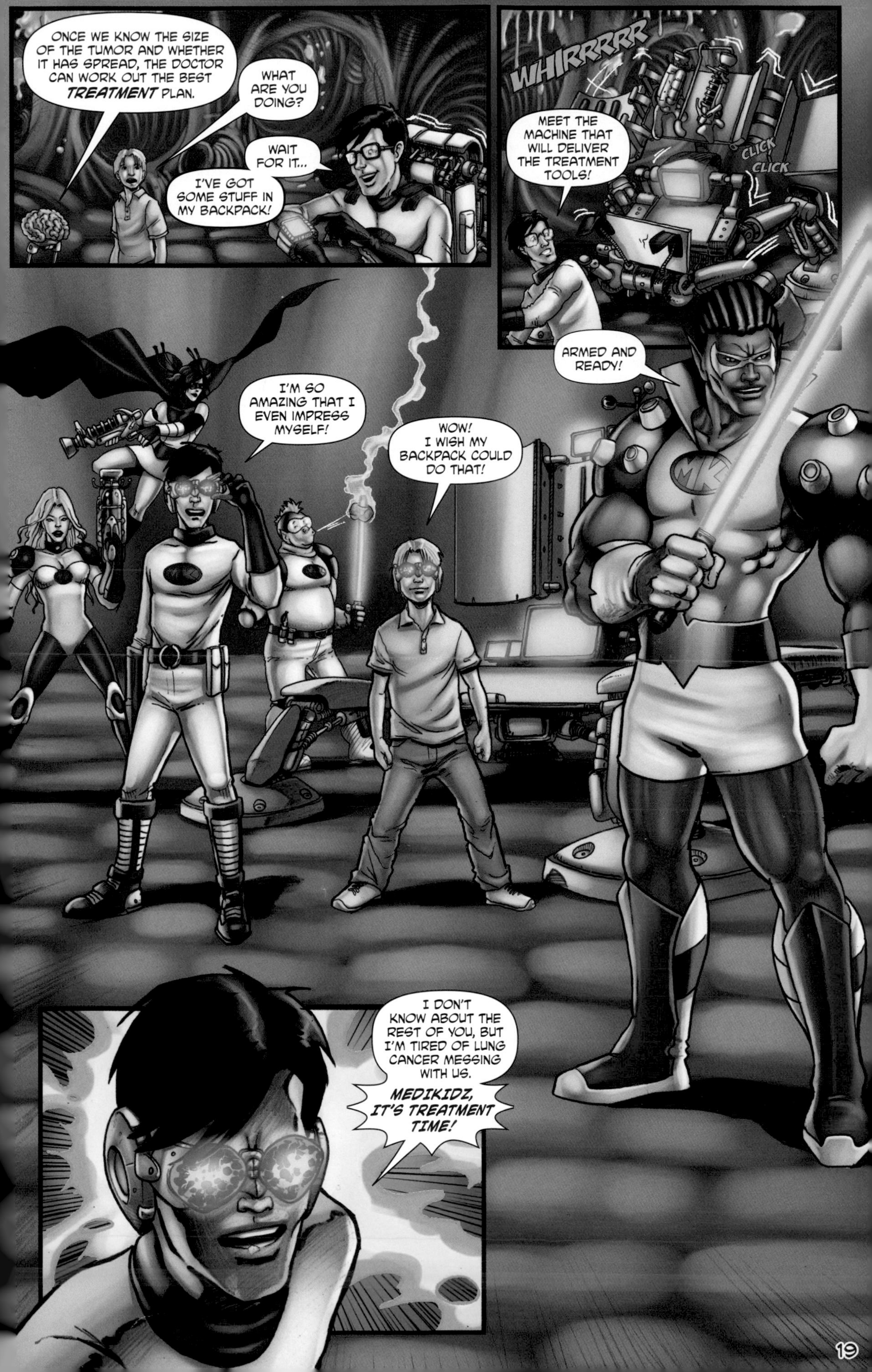
ONCE WE KNOW THE SIZE OF THE TUMOR AND WHETHER IT HAS SPREAD, THE DOCTOR CAN WORK OUT THE BEST TREATMENT PLAN.
WHAT ARE YOU DOING?
WAIT FOR IT...
I'VE GOT SOME STUFF IN MY BACKPACK!
WHIRRRRR
MEET THE MACHINE THAT WILL DELIVER THE TREATMENT TOOLS!
CLICK
CLICK
ARMED AND READY!
I'M SO AMAZING THAT I EVEN IMPRESS MYSELF!
WOW! I WISH MY BACKPACK COULD DO THAT!
I DON'T KNOW ABOUT THE REST OF YOU, BUT I'M TIRED OF LUNG CANCER MESSING WITH US.
MEDIKIDZ, IT'S TREATMENT TIME!

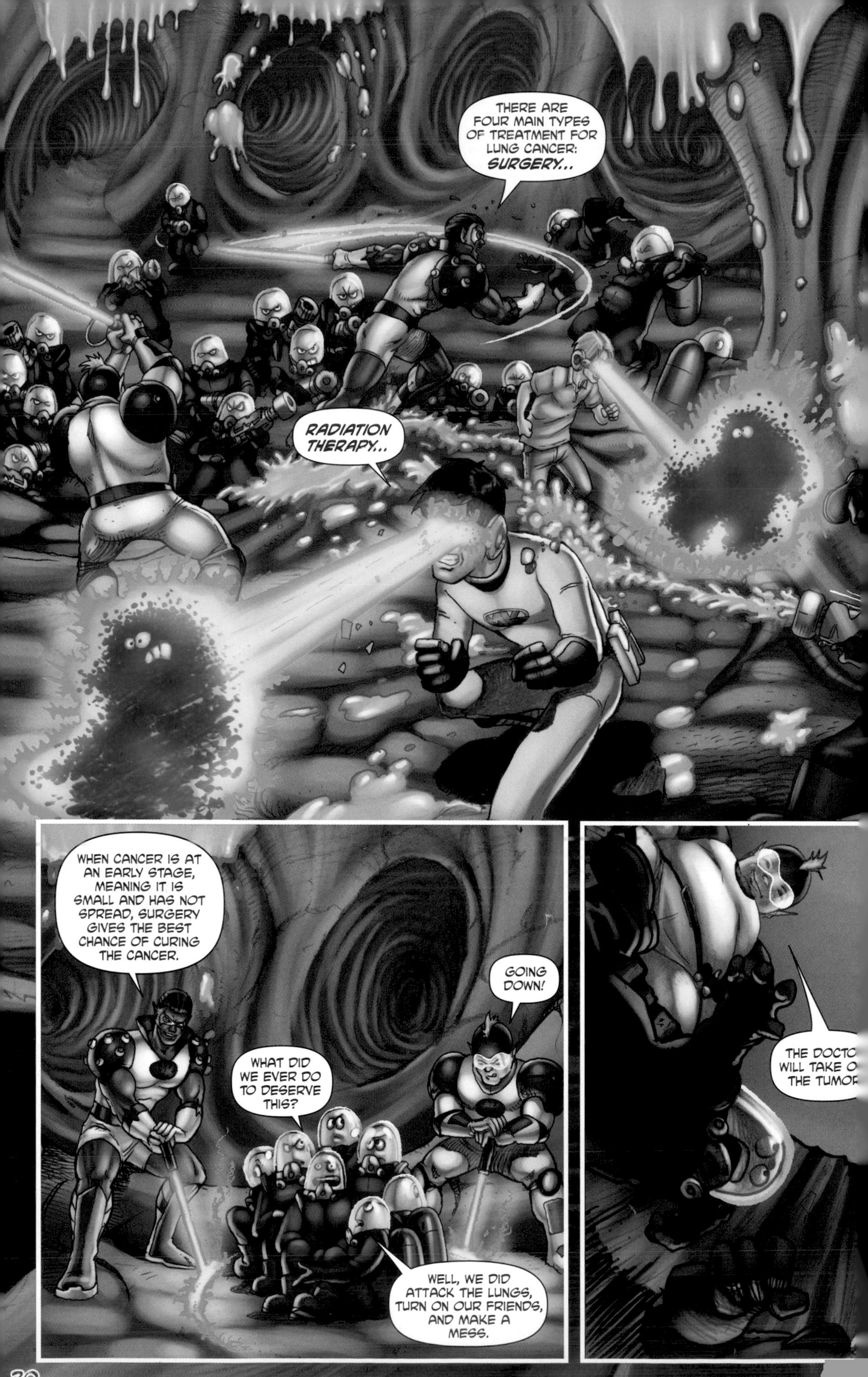

THERE ARE FOUR MAIN TYPES OF TREATMENT FOR LUNG CANCER: SURGERY...
RADIATION THERAPY...
WHEN CANCER IS AT AN EARLY STAGE, MEANING IT IS SMALL AND HAS NOT SPREAD, SURGERY GIVES THE BEST CHANCE OF CURING THE CANCER.
GOING DOWN!
WHAT DID WE EVER DO TO DESERVE THIS?
WELL, WE DID ATTACK THE LUNGS, TURN ON OUR FRIENDS, AND MAKE A MESS.
THE DOCTO WILL TAKE O THE TUMOR

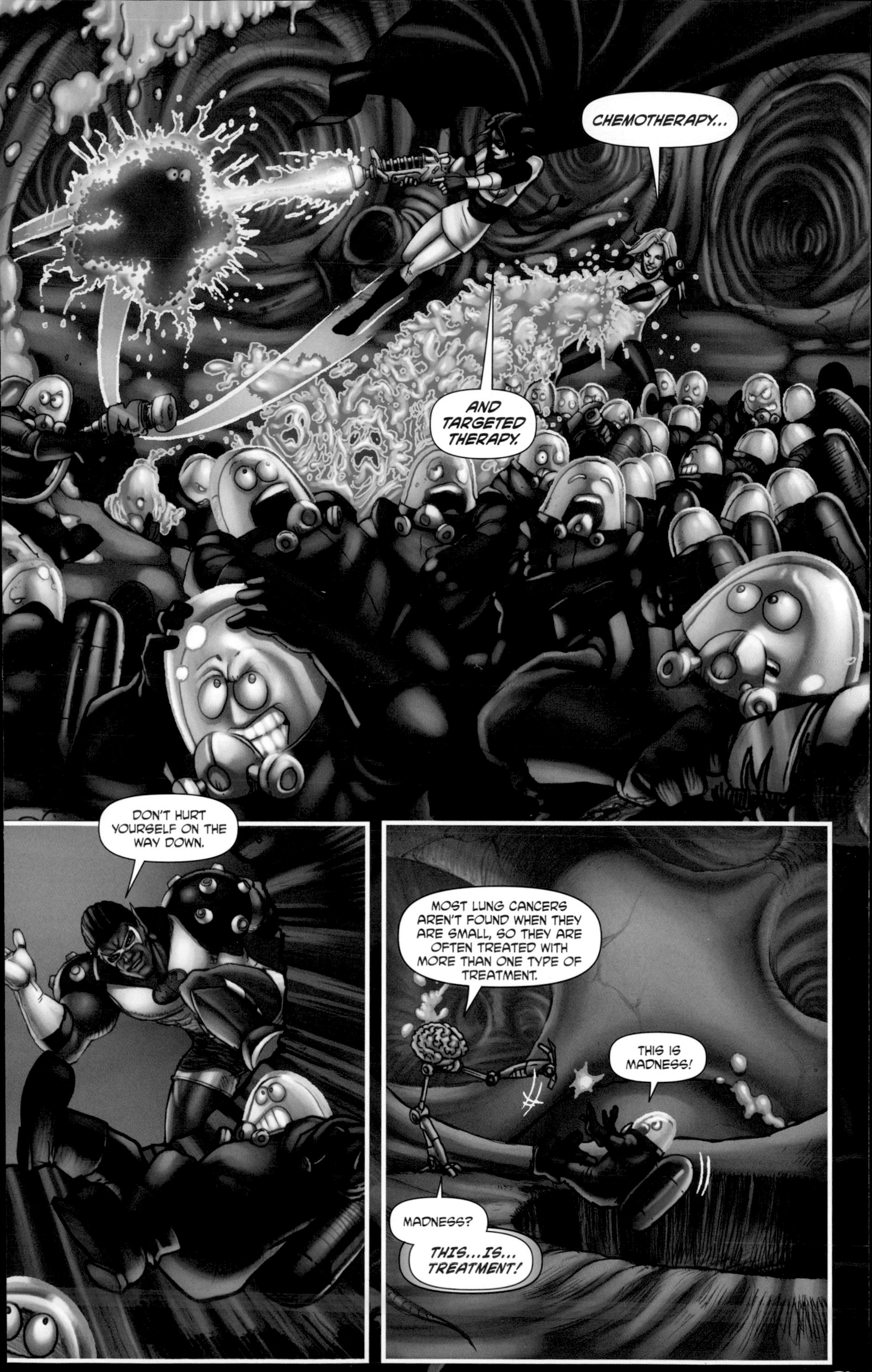
CHEMOTHERAPY...
AND TARGETED THERAPY.
DON'T HURT YOURSELF ON THE WAY DOWN.
MOST LUNG CANCERS AREN'T FOUND WHEN THEY ARE SMALL, SO THEY ARE OFTEN TREATED WITH MORE THAN ONE TYPE OF TREATMENT.
THIS IS MADNESS!
MADNESS?
THIS...IS... TREATMENT!

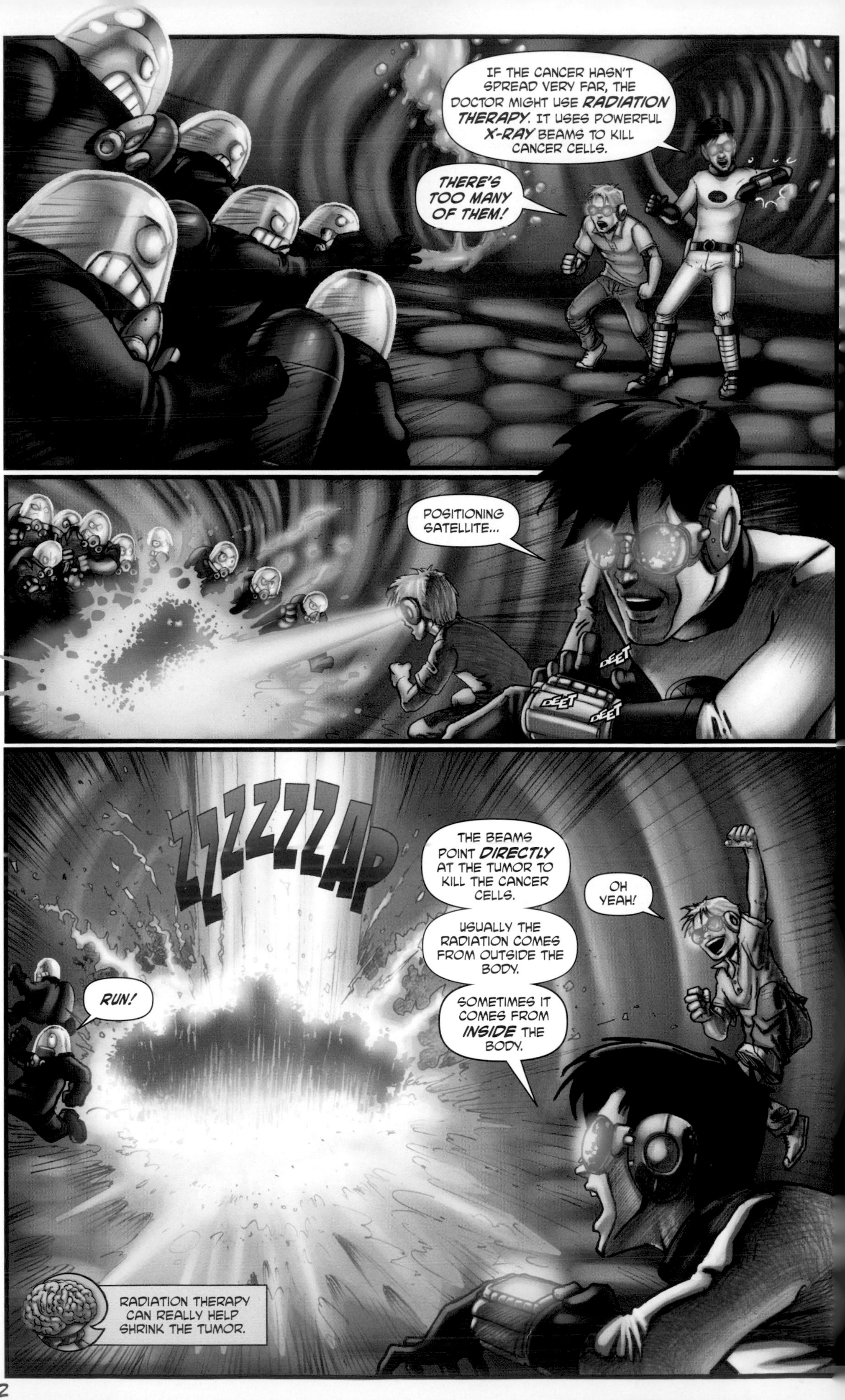
IF THE CANCER HASN'T SPREAD VERY FAR, THE DOCTOR MIGHT USE RADIATION THERAPY. IT USES POWERFUL X-RAY BEAMS TO KILL CANCER CELLS.
THERE'S TOO MANY OF THEM!
POSITIONING SATELLITE...
DEET
DEET
DEET
DEET
ZZZZZZAP
THE BEAMS POINT DIRECTLY AT THE TUMOR TO KILL THE CANCER CELLS.
USUALLY THE RADIATION COMES FROM OUTSIDE THE BODY.
SOMETIMES IT COMES FROM INSIDE THE BODY.
OH YEAH!
RUN!
RADIATION THERAPY CAN REALLY HELP SHRINK THE TUMOR.

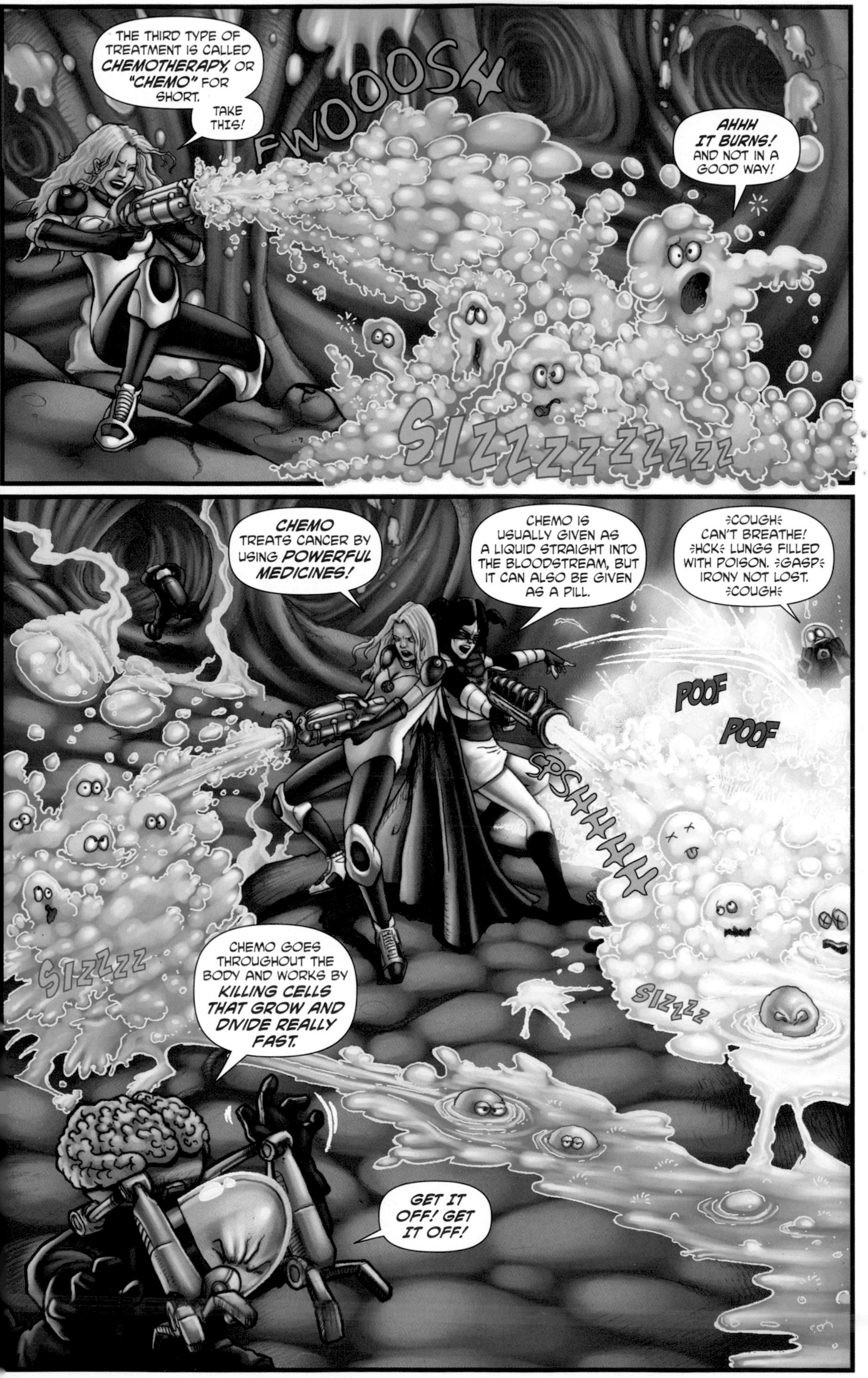

THE THIRD TYPE OF TREATMENT IS CALLED CHEMOTHERAPY, OR "CHEMO" FOR SHORT.
TAKE THIS!
FWOOOSH
AHHH IT BURNS! AND NOT IN A GOOD WAY!
SIZZZZZZZZZZ
CHEMO TREATS CANCER BY USING POWERFUL MEDICINES!
CHEMO IS USUALLY GIVEN AS A LIQUID STRAIGHT INTO THE BLOODSTREAM, BUT IT CAN ALSO BE GIVEN AS A PILL.
COUGH CAN'T BREATHE! *HCK* LUNGS FILLED WITH POISON. *GASP* IRONY NOT LOST. *COUGH*
POOF
POOF
SPSHHHHH
SIZZZZ
CHEMO GOES THROUGHOUT THE BODY AND WORKS BY KILLING CELLS THAT GROW AND DIVIDE REALLY FAST.
SIZZZZ
GET IT OFF! GET IT OFF!

CHEMO ALSO AFFECTS OTHER HEALTHY CELLS THAT NORMALLY GROW FAST. THIS CAN CAUSE *SIDE EFFECTS.*

SIDE EFFECTS ARE WHEN MEDICINES DO THINGS OTHER THAN WHAT THE DOCTOR WANTS THEM TO DO.

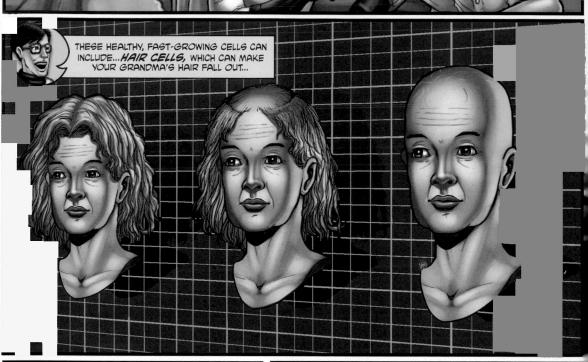

THESE HEALTHY, FAST-GROWING CELLS CAN INCLUDE...*HAIR CELLS,* WHICH CAN MAKE YOUR GRANDMA'S HAIR FALL OUT...

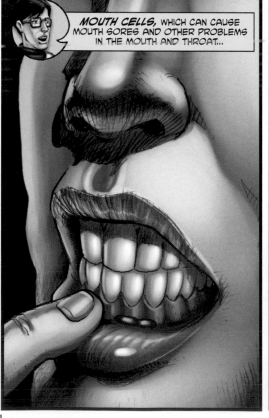

MOUTH CELLS, WHICH CAN CAUSE MOUTH SORES AND OTHER PROBLEMS IN THE MOUTH AND THROAT...

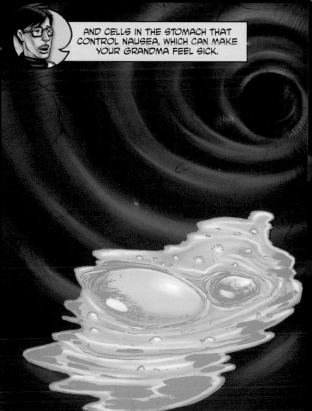

AND CELLS IN THE STOMACH THAT CONTROL NAUSEA, WHICH CAN MAKE YOUR GRANDMA FEEL SICK.

24

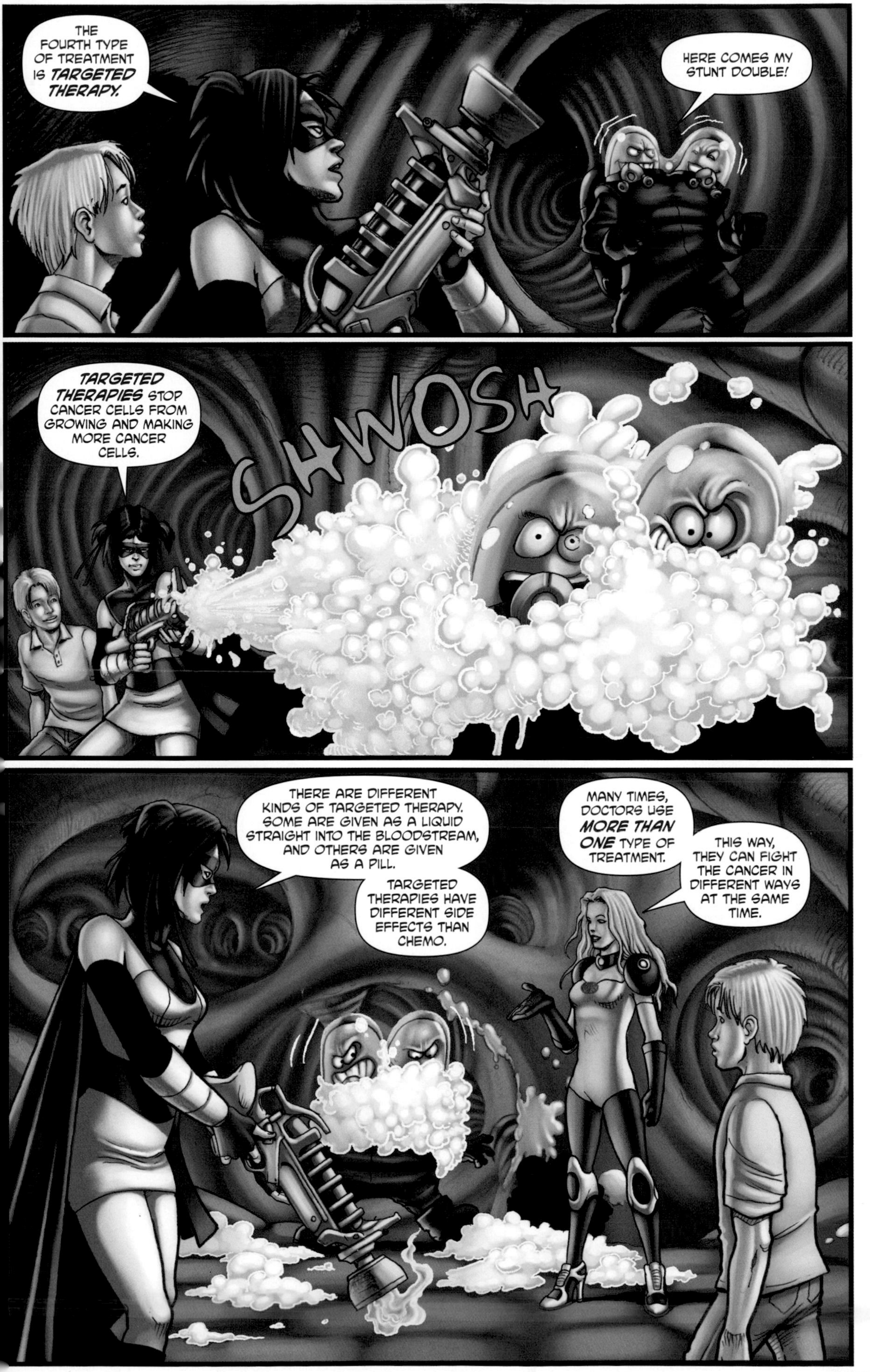
THE FOURTH TYPE OF TREATMENT IS TARGETED THERAPY.
HERE COMES MY STUNT DOUBLE!
TARGETED THERAPIES STOP CANCER CELLS FROM GROWING AND MAKING MORE CANCER CELLS.
SHWOSH
THERE ARE DIFFERENT KINDS OF TARGETED THERAPY. SOME ARE GIVEN AS A LIQUID STRAIGHT INTO THE BLOODSTREAM, AND OTHERS ARE GIVEN AS A PILL.
TARGETED THERAPIES HAVE DIFFERENT SIDE EFFECTS THAN CHEMO.
MANY TIMES, DOCTORS USE MORE THAN ONE TYPE OF TREATMENT.
THIS WAY, THEY CAN FIGHT THE CANCER IN DIFFERENT WAYS AT THE SAME TIME.

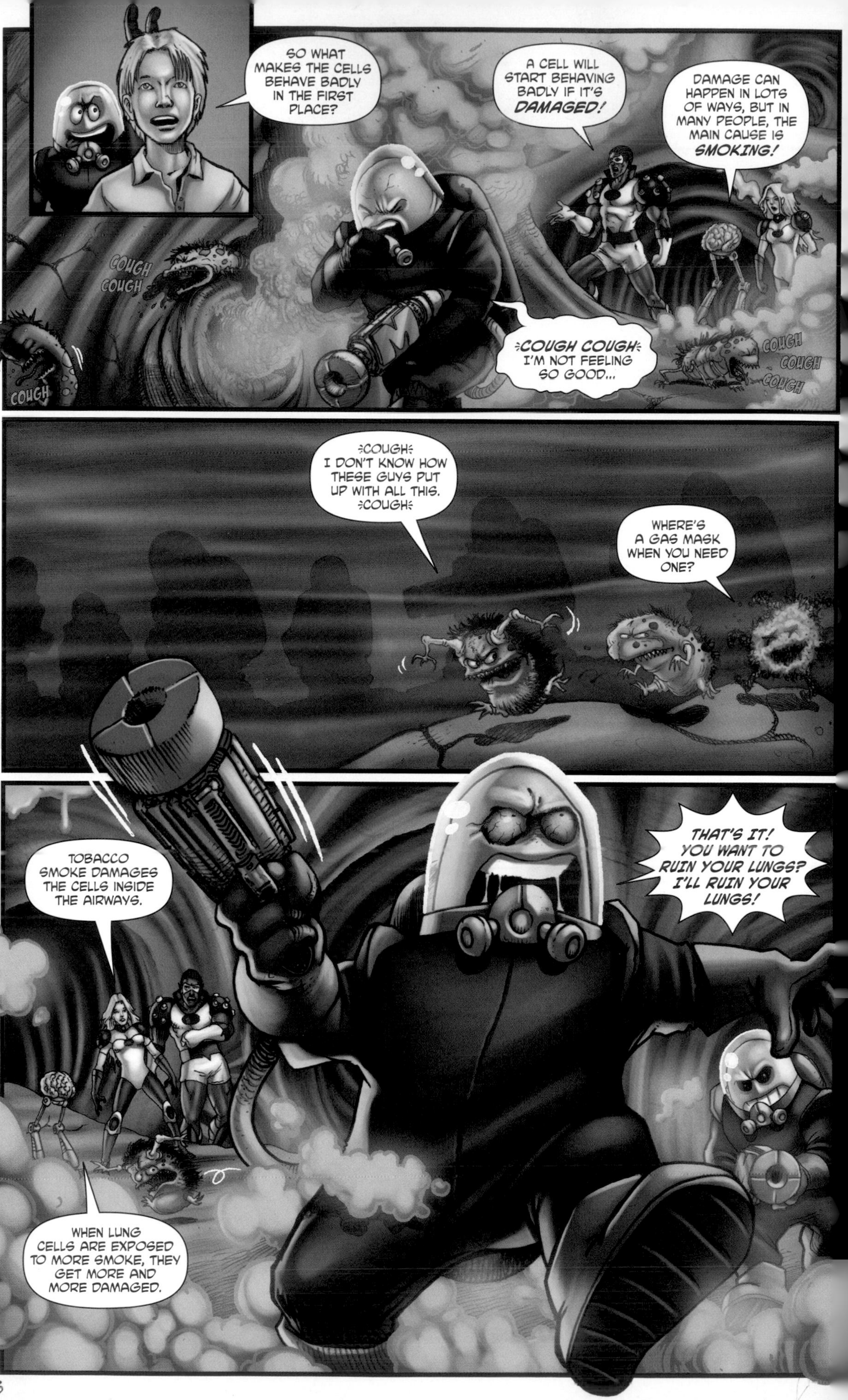
SO WHAT MAKES THE CELLS BEHAVE BADLY IN THE FIRST PLACE?
A CELL WILL START BEHAVING BADLY IF IT'S DAMAGED!
DAMAGE CAN HAPPEN IN LOTS OF WAYS, BUT IN MANY PEOPLE, THE MAIN CAUSE IS SMOKING!
COUGH COUGH
COUGH
COUGH COUGH I'M NOT FEELING SO GOOD...
COUGH COUGH COUGH
COUGH I DON'T KNOW HOW THESE GUYS PUT UP WITH ALL THIS. COUGH
WHERE'S A GAS MASK WHEN YOU NEED ONE?
TOBACCO SMOKE DAMAGES THE CELLS INSIDE THE AIRWAYS.
THAT'S IT! YOU WANT TO RUIN YOUR LUNGS? I'LL RUIN YOUR LUNGS!
WHEN LUNG CELLS ARE EXPOSED TO MORE SMOKE, THEY GET MORE AND MORE DAMAGED.

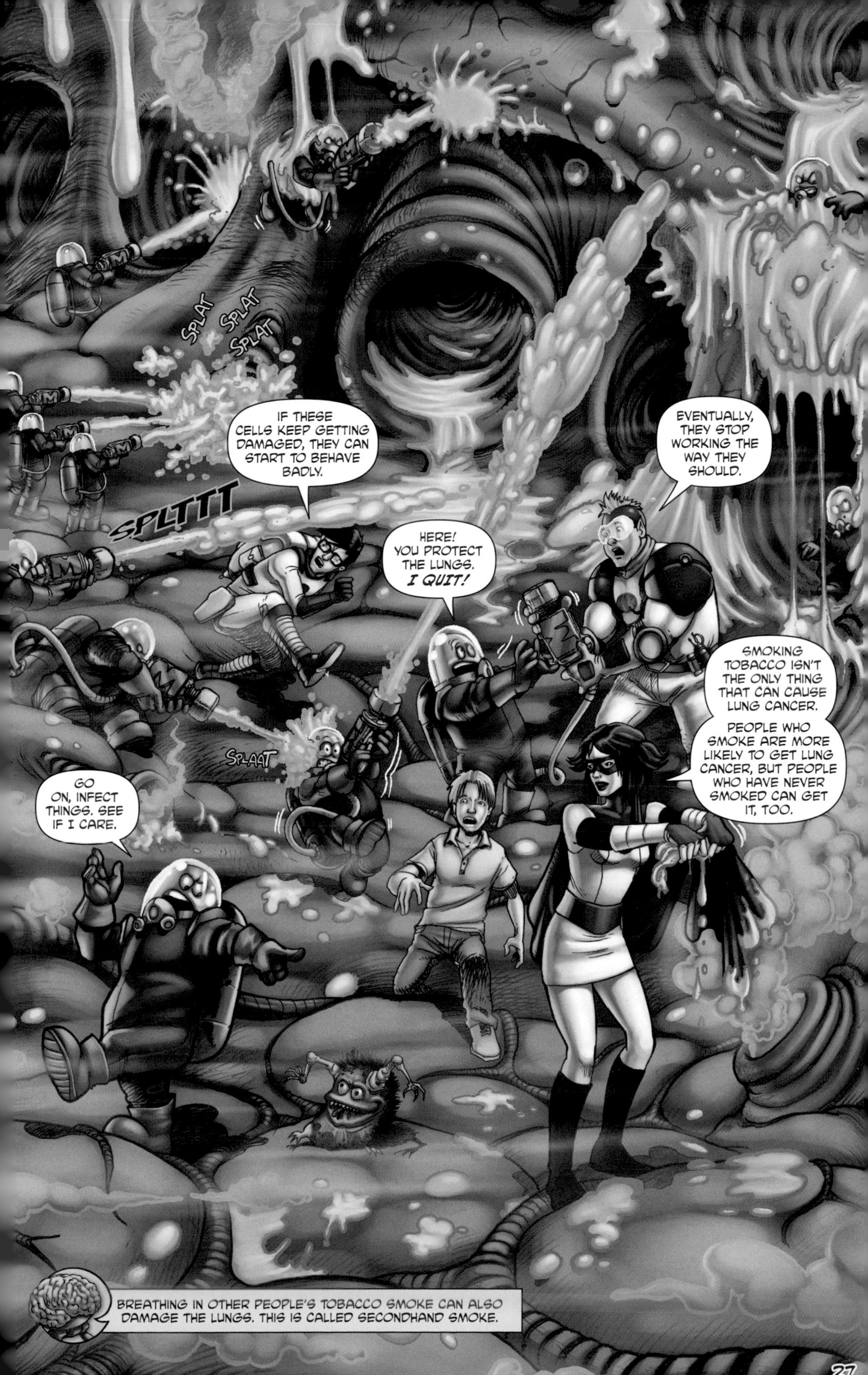
SPLAT
SPLAT
SPLAT
IF THESE CELLS KEEP GETTING DAMAGED, THEY CAN START TO BEHAVE BADLY.
EVENTUALLY, THEY STOP WORKING THE WAY THEY SHOULD.
SPLTTT
HERE! YOU PROTECT THE LUNGS. *I QUIT!*
SMOKING TOBACCO ISN'T THE ONLY THING THAT CAN CAUSE LUNG CANCER.
PEOPLE WHO SMOKE ARE MORE LIKELY TO GET LUNG CANCER, BUT PEOPLE WHO HAVE NEVER SMOKED CAN GET IT, TOO.
SPLAAT
GO ON, INFECT THINGS. SEE IF I CARE.
BREATHING IN OTHER PEOPLE'S TOBACCO SMOKE CAN ALSO DAMAGE THE LUNGS. THIS IS CALLED SECONDHAND SMOKE.

SO LET ME SEE WHETHER I'VE GOT THIS RIGHT. FIRST, THE CELLS IN THE LUNGS ARE DAMAGED AND START TO **BEHAVE BADLY.**

THESE BAD CELLS GROW REALLY QUICKLY, BLOCKING THE AIRWAYS, WHICH CAN MAKE IT HARD FOR MY GRAMDMA TO BREATHE. THIS CAN ALSO MAKE HER COUGH A LOT.

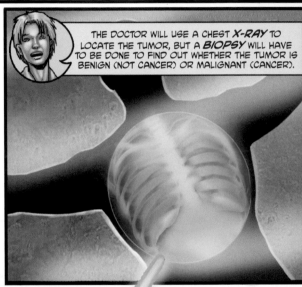

THE DOCTOR WILL USE A CHEST **X-RAY** TO LOCATE THE TUMOR, BUT A **BIOPSY** WILL HAVE TO BE DONE TO FIND OUT WHETHER THE TUMOR IS BENIGN (NOT CANCER) OR MALIGNANT (CANCER).

IF THE TUMOR IS SMALL AND HASN'T SPREAD, THEN **SURGERY** IS USUALLY PART OF THE FIRST TREATMENT.

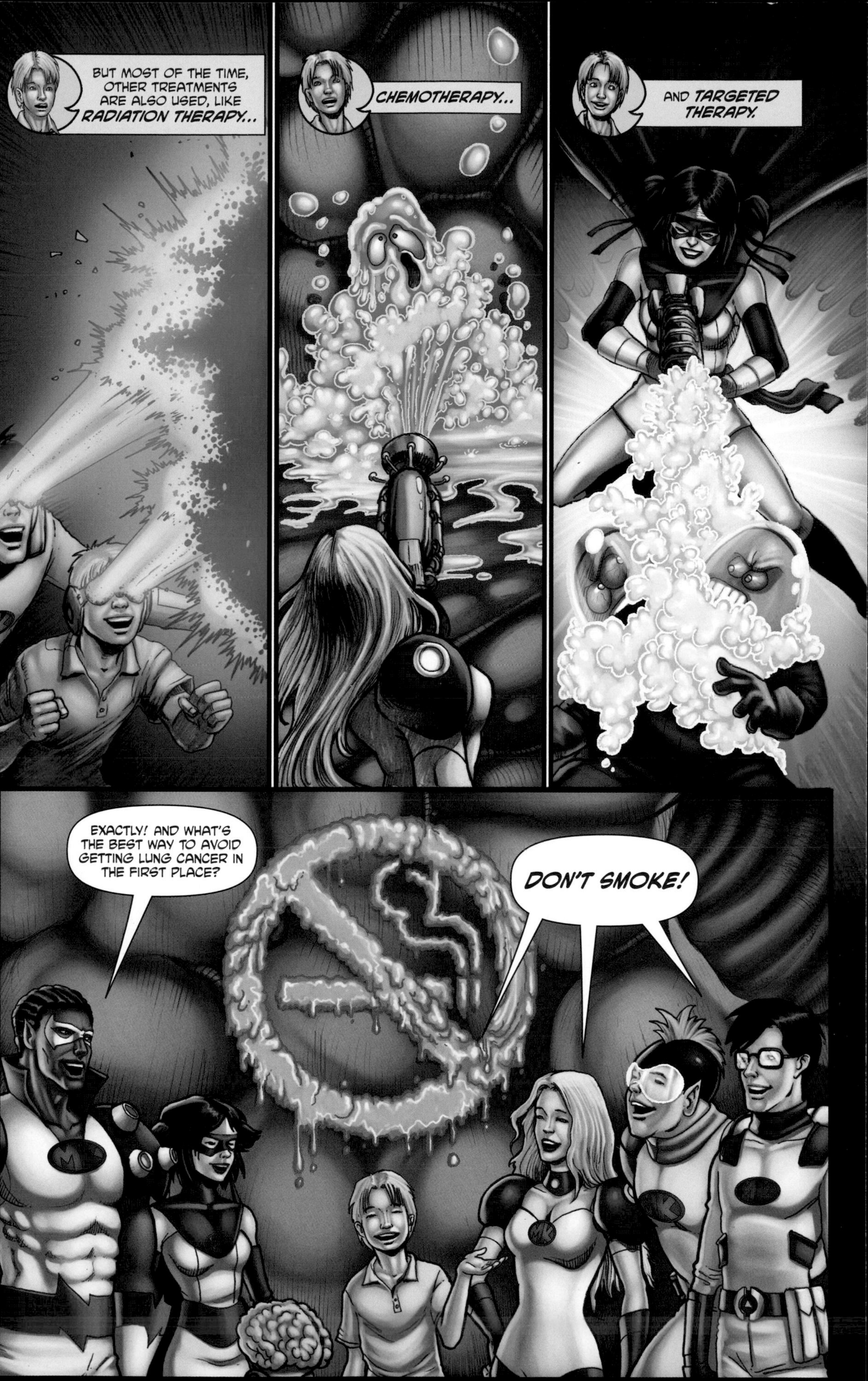
BUT MOST OF THE TIME, OTHER TREATMENTS ARE ALSO USED, LIKE RADIATION THERAPY...
CHEMOTHERAPY...
AND TARGETED THERAPY.
EXACTLY! AND WHAT'S THE BEST WAY TO AVOID GETTING LUNG CANCER IN THE FIRST PLACE?
DON'T SMOKE!

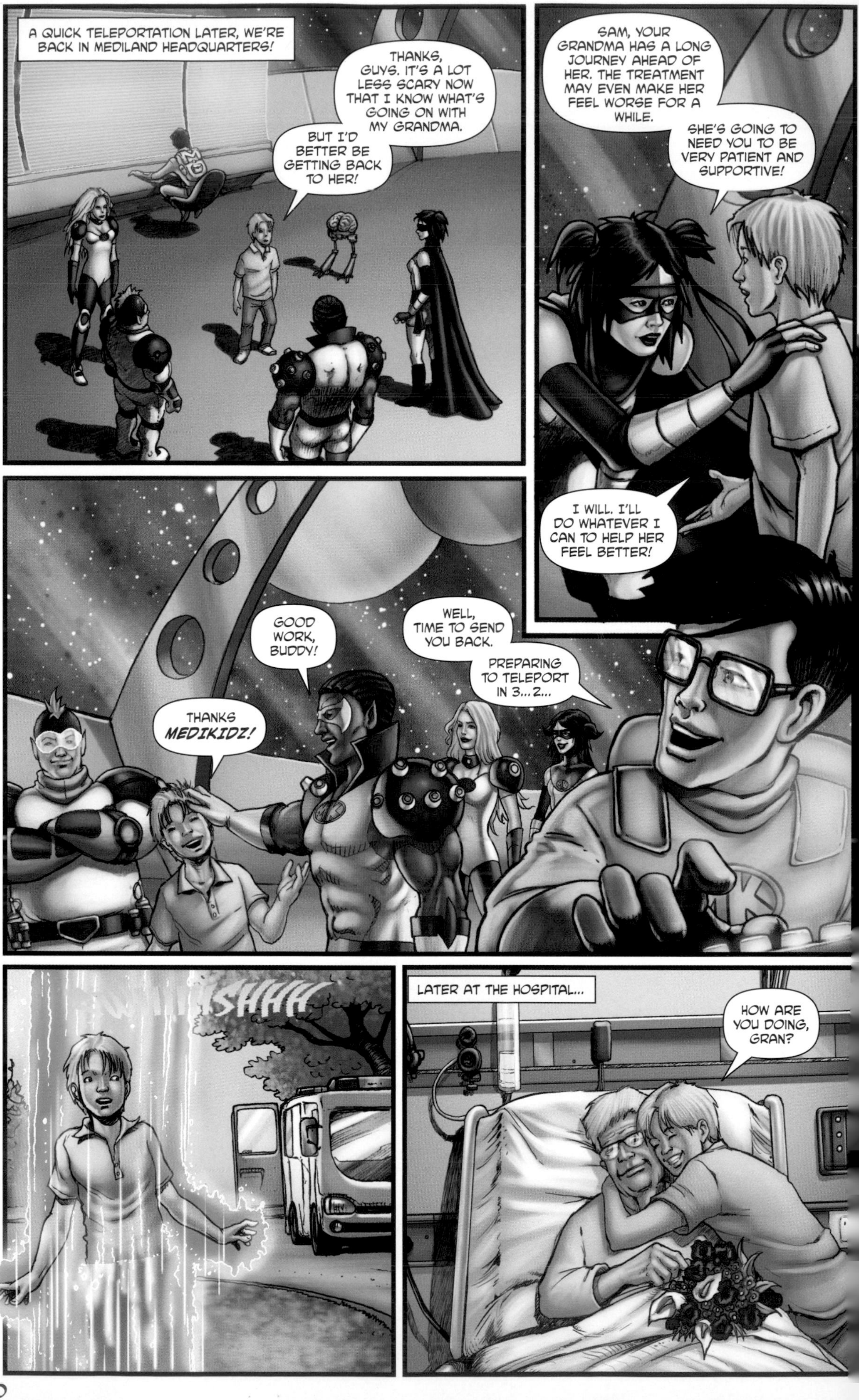
A QUICK TELEPORTATION LATER, WE'RE BACK IN MEDILAND HEADQUARTERS!
THANKS, GUYS. IT'S A LOT LESS SCARY NOW THAT I KNOW WHAT'S GOING ON WITH MY GRANDMA.
BUT I'D BETTER BE GETTING BACK TO HER!
SAM, YOUR GRANDMA HAS A LONG JOURNEY AHEAD OF HER. THE TREATMENT MAY EVEN MAKE HER FEEL WORSE FOR A WHILE.
SHE'S GOING TO NEED YOU TO BE VERY PATIENT AND SUPPORTIVE!
I WILL. I'LL DO WHATEVER I CAN TO HELP HER FEEL BETTER!
GOOD WORK, BUDDY!
THANKS *MEDIKIDZ!*
WELL, TIME TO SEND YOU BACK.
PREPARING TO TELEPORT IN 3... 2...
SHHH
LATER AT THE HOSPITAL...
HOW ARE YOU DOING, GRAN?

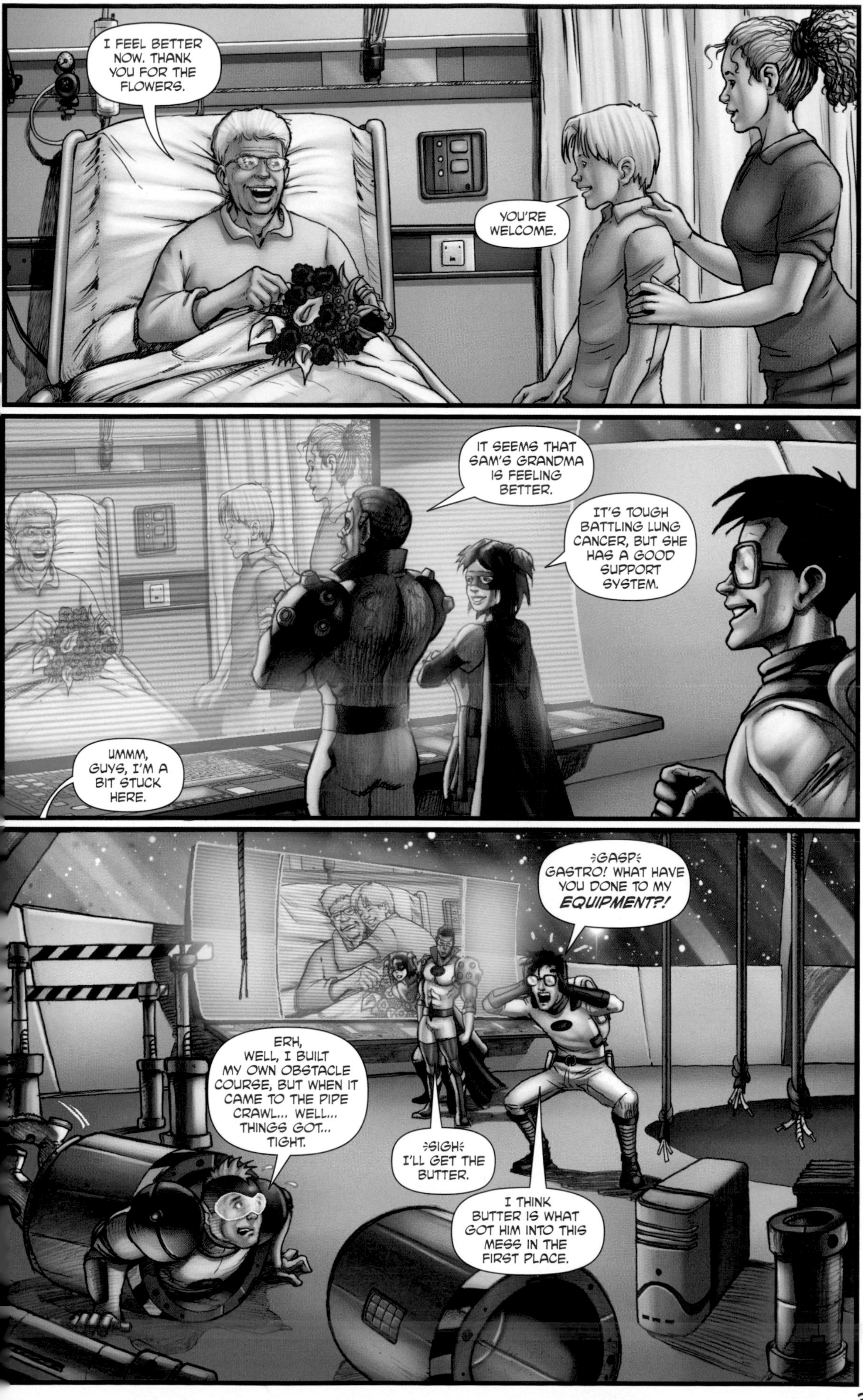
I FEEL BETTER NOW. THANK YOU FOR THE FLOWERS.
YOU'RE WELCOME.
IT SEEMS THAT SAM'S GRANDMA IS FEELING BETTER.
IT'S TOUGH BATTLING LUNG CANCER, BUT SHE HAS A GOOD SUPPORT SYSTEM.
UMMM, GUYS, I'M A BIT STUCK HERE.
GASP GASTRO! WHAT HAVE YOU DONE TO MY *EQUIPMENT?!*
ERH, WELL, I BUILT MY OWN OBSTACLE COURSE, BUT WHEN IT CAME TO THE PIPE CRAWL... WELL... THINGS GOT... TIGHT.
SIGH I'LL GET THE BUTTER.
I THINK BUTTER IS WHAT GOT HIM INTO THIS MESS IN THE FIRST PLACE.

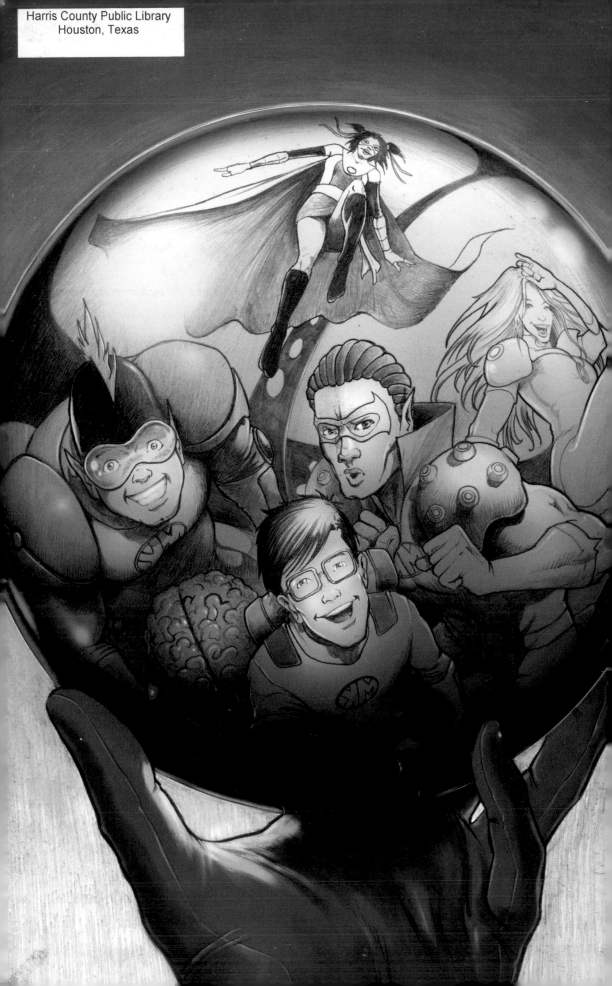